Springtime for the Soul

A LENTEN DEVOTIONAL

MEL SHOEMAKER

WESTBOW
PRESS®
A DIVISION OF THOMAS NELSON
& ZONDERVAN

New Revised Standard Version Bible, copyright 1989, Division of Christian
Education of the National Council of the Churches of Christ in the
United States of America. Used by permission. All rights reserved.

WestBow Press books may be ordered through booksellers or by contacting:

WestBow Press
A Division of Thomas Nelson & Zondervan
1663 Liberty Drive
Bloomington, IN 47403
www.westbowpress.com
1 (866) 928-1240

ISBN: 978-1-5127-5698-2 (sc)
ISBN: 978-1-5127-5700-2 (hc)
ISBN: 978-1-5127-5699-9 (e)

Library of Congress Control Number: 2016915362

Print information available on the last page.

WestBow Press rev. date: 09/27/2016

About the Author

Rev. Dr. Melvin H. Shoemaker (M Div, M Phil, D Min) was professor of New Testament biblical literature and theology in the School of Theology at Azusa Pacific University, Azusa, California, from 1986 to 2005. Previously, he was professor of religion at Oklahoma Wesleyan University, Bartlesville, Oklahoma, and Indiana Wesleyan University, Marion, Indiana. He is an ordained minister in the Wesleyan Church and served as a parish minister for twenty years. He is the author of *The Theology of the Four Gospels* (WestBow Press, 2011) and *Good News for Today: A Lenten Devotional* (WestBow Press, 2013) and a contributor to numerous anthologies, dictionaries, and scholarly journals in biblical literature and theology. Dr. Shoemaker retired in 2005 and now resides in Portland, Oregon.

To All God's Beloved

"The gifts Christ gave were ... to equip the saints for the work of ministry, for building up the body of Christ, until all of us come to the unity of the faith and of the knowledge of the Son of God, to maturity, to the measure of the full stature of Christ. We must no longer be children, tossed to and fro and blown about by every wind of doctrine ... But speaking the truth in love, we must grow up in every way into him who is the head, into Christ." (Eph. 4:11–15)

Contents

Week Four

Week Five

Week Six

Week Seven—Passion Week

Preface

Lent has the historic, root meaning of spring, springtime, and the lengthening of the days. In the days of winter, following the December solstice and the shortest day of light in the Northern Hemisphere, there is a longing for spring—a longing for the lengthening of days, more sunshine, warmer temperatures, less frost and bone-chilling cold. Long evenings are occupied with reading, television, movies, puzzles, texting family and friends, and Internet searches. Whereas our grandparents and parents anticipated the January arrival of the seed catalogs, modern gardeners search the Internet for seeds, bulbs, shrubs, trees, and new landscaping ideas. The long evenings are filled with hope and visions of what can be—what will be with a plan, hard work, and God's season of springtime.

Lent has been observed by Christians as the "season of springtime for the soul." That certainly is a positive twist on Lent. Commonly, the first thought that comes to mind is a season of penitence and fasting from Ash Wednesday to Easter. Too frequently, the somber aspect of abstinence, self-discipline, reflection, and introspection have so dominated our observance of Lent that we want Mardi Gras to never end. But February is here, and it is once again that time of the year for Christians to observe Lent.

Springtime for the Soul: A Lenten Devotional is a series of readings and meditations composed for Christians—God's holy ones, saints— who are on a quest to grow and gain a greater understanding of our faith. It is my purpose and hope that you will find the daily readings and the meditations refreshing and encouraging, cultivating the crusty, winter soil of the heart and germinating new thoughts concerning the essentials of our living faith.

What are the essentials of our faith? The forty-seven devotionals that follow attempt to address and answer that question. They invite us to remember, review, and renew our Christian confession. The apostle Peter wrote this timely appeal to the early church: "This is now, beloved, the second letter I am writing to you; in them I am trying to arouse your sincere intention by reminding you that you should remember the words spoken in the past by the holy prophets, and the commandment of the Lord and Savior spoken through your apostles" (2 Pet. 3:1f). Remember! Too often, we forget. The essentials include the covenant, the commandments, the canon of scripture, prayer, and the concise confession of the essentials passed from generation to generation in the historic, ecumenical creeds of the church.

Based upon the historic tradition of the lectionary, there are three readings of scripture each day, which relate to the subject or theme of the day. Instead of the traditional three readings in the Old Testament, Psalms, and New Testament, the Old Testament reading has been replaced by what is called "First Reading." Frequently in this devotional series, both the "first" and "second" reading may be in the New Testament scriptures. Therefore, both the first and second readings are significantly relevant for the meditation that follows.

Therefore, you, the reader, may choose one of three optional devotional plans in the use of this book, depending upon the time you may have each day.

Plan 1—Read First Reading, Psalm, Second Reading, and the meditation for the day (fifteen minutes).

Plan 2—Read First Reading, Second Reading, and the meditation for the day (thirteen minutes).

Plan 3—Read Second Reading and the meditation for the day (ten minutes).

The scripture readings provide the seed from which the meditation germinates, sprouts, and grows.

It is my prayer and purpose that we will remember, review, and renew our confession in the Lord, our God. Let us together covenant to make this Lent springtime for our souls.

Mel Shoemaker
2016

FOUNDATIONS OF A LIVING FAITH

Springtime for the Soul

First Reading:	2 Pet. 1:1–15; 3:1–2
Poetry and Wisdom:	Ps. 103:1–14
Second Reading:	Luke 24:1–12

"Remember how he told you, while he was still in Galilee, that the Son of Man must be handed over to sinners, and be crucified, and on the third day rise again." (Luke 24:6–7)[1]

―――――――――

Ash Wednesday marks the beginning of Lent, the season of preparation for our Lord's passion on Good Friday and anticipation of his Easter resurrection. Many Christians throughout the world will fast and assemble today in solemn worship and have the sign of the cross drawn on their foreheads with ashes. Some pastors or priests may say, "Remember that you are dust, and to dust you shall return" (Gen. 3:19), while others may say, "Repent and believe the gospel" (Mark 1:15). The ashes signify repentance and sorrow for our sins before a holy and merciful God (e.g., Jon. 3:5f). They present a somber reminder of life's brevity and our ultimate accountability to our creator and judge.

Remember! This is a frequent exhortation in the scriptures. Moses called upon Israel to remember. "Remember that you were a slave in the land of Egypt, and the LORD your God brought you out from there with a mighty hand and an outstretched arm" (Deut. 5:15). "Remember the long way that the LORD your God has led you these forty years in the wilderness, in order to humble you, testing you to know what was in your heart, whether or not you would keep his commandments" (Deut. 8:2). "Remember that you were a slave in the land of Egypt, and the LORD your God redeemed you" (Deut. 15:15). Therefore, ancient Israel and Jews to this day remember God's deliverance and the exodus in the annual observance of the Passover.

Passover could fall on any day of the week. However, according to John, Jesus was crucified and died on the day of Preparation for a particularly holy Passover, a Sabbath day of "great solemnity" (John 19:31). This note implies that the Passover that year coincided with the Sabbath, the seventh day of the week. In other words, the Passover was a fixed holy day in the Jewish lunar calendar and not a fixed day in the week.

On the fourteenth day of the first month of the Jewish lunar calendar, the day of Preparation for the Passover (Mark 15:42; John 19:14), a lamb or goat was slaughtered in the afternoon. In the evening after sunset, which marks the beginning of Passover, the sacrificial animal was roasted and eaten with unleavened bread and bitter herbs (Exod. 12:1–20; Lev. 23:5–8; Num. 28:16–25). It was a holy day of remembrance.

Setting the date for the Jewish Passover, and therefore Good Friday and Easter, initially would seem quite simple. This conclusion, however, is not the case. Determining the date of Good Friday and Easter has caused many disputes and even historic schisms in the church. In part, the problem is caused by the calendars—Jewish, Julian, and Gregorian. In general, Christians, beginning in the fourth century, abandoned the custom of relying upon the full moon of the Jewish Passover. Subsequently, the Western church adopted the Gregorian calendar, while the Eastern church retained the older Julian calendar. Whereas the early church observed the holy days in relationship with the Passover, currently Easter in the West may occur on a Sunday between March 22 and April 25. In the Eastern Orthodox churches, Easter is usually later.

Therefore there is only a loose association between the date of the vernal or spring equinox, the Jewish Passover, the Christian observance of Good Friday, and the celebration of Easter. The first day of spring is an astronomical event, the day in which the plane determined by the earth's equator passes through the center of the sun. The length of day and night—light and darkness—is equal on that day. Beginning with the spring equinox, in the Northern Hemisphere the daylight hours lengthen a few minutes each day until the longest day of the year—that is, the summer solstice, which is the first day of summer.[2]

Good Friday is the Christian "Passover," our day of remembrance. It is the day on which Jesus, the Lamb of God, was crucified and died to take away the sin of the world (John 1:29). Crucifixion is a gory business—capital punishment at its worst—and was reserved for the most hideous of crimes in the Roman Empire. Jesus suffered crucifixion and death for the forgiveness of our sins, both yours and mine. Remember, this is the good news of the gospel, the forgiveness of sins (Matt. 26:27; Luke 22:19, 24:46; 1 Cor. 11:24–25).

Lent is the season of preparation for Good Friday and the anticipation of Easter. Remember, there can be no Easter joy without the plowing and cultivation of the crusty winter soil; no Easter joy without heavenly rains to soften the earth; and no Easter joy without the planting of seed, death, and dying. This is the noble purpose of these Lenten readings and meditations. They aspire to renew the mind and inspire the heart with reminders and fresh insights into the essentials of our faith. Remember, Lent is springtime for the soul.

Prayer:
It is my prayer, blessed Spirit of truth, that these forty days of Lent shall be a season of plowing and cultivating the soil of my heart through the reading of scripture and meditation upon the words spoken by Moses, the prophets, Christ our Lord, and the apostles.
Please send your rain and plant new seed in this springtime for my soul. Amen.

[1] Cf. Mark 8:31, 9:31, 10:33–34; Matt. 16:21, 17:22, 20:18–19; and Luke 9:22, 18:32–33.

[2] In 2017, the vernal or spring equinox will occur on Monday, March 20, followed by the Passover beginning at sunset on the full moon, Monday, April 10, which is twenty-one days after the beginning of spring. Passover and Good Friday will occur within the same week, and Easter Sunday will follow on April 16, 2017.

The Tree of Life

First Reading: Gen. 3:1–24
Poetry and Wisdom: Prov. 3:13–18
Second Reading: Rev. 2:7; 21:1–5, 22–27; 22:1–5, 12–14

"Blessed are those who wash their robes, so that they will have the right to the tree of life and may enter the city by the gates." (Rev. 22:14)

Many insurrectionists and murderers died on Roman crosses in the first century; in fact, as many as two thousand revolutionaries were crucified at one time in 4 BC (Josephus, *Antiquities* 17.10.10). But only one was buried and raised, leaving an empty tomb. That makes Jesus's cross both unique and a universal symbol of our Christian faith.

The English term "cross," however, creates a misunderstanding, for it creates the image of a pole having a crossbeam forming an X in some fashion. The Latin *crux*, the Greek σταυρός, and the Hebrew עֵץ ['ēṣ] may refer to a tree, pole, stake, or simply a piece of wood.

John 3:14 recalls a difficult time in the wilderness wanderings of Israel during the Exodus, stating, "Just as Moses lifted up the serpent in the wilderness, so must the Son of Man be lifted up, that whoever believes in him may have eternal life." Many of the Israelites had died from the bites of poisonous snakes. After Moses had confessed the sins of the people, he prayed that God would take away the serpents. At the Lord's instruction, Moses fashioned a bronze serpent on a "pole." Thus, "Whenever a serpent bit someone, that person would look at the serpent of bronze and live" (Num. 21:9). That pole or tree became a tree of life to Israel.

God planted a plethora of beautiful, fruitful trees in the Garden of Eden to provide healthy food to our first parents. However, only two trees were specifically named, the "tree of life" and the "tree of the knowledge of good and evil" (Gen. 2:9). There was only one limiting stipulation. God commanded them, "You may freely eat of every tree of the garden; but of the tree of the knowledge of good and evil you shall not eat, for in the day that you eat of it you shall die" (Gen. 2:16f). For many, the tree of life is forgotten in the story. Yes, the woman and the man both ate of the forbidden fruit of the tree of the knowledge of good and evil. Therefore they and all their descendants began experiencing the critical curse of their sin —death, that is.

No, Adam and Eve did not die immediately, but they began to die. They now understood right from wrong, and God pronounced his judgment: "[Lest] he might [continue to] reach out his hand and take also from the tree of life, and eat, and live forever" (Gen. 3:22), sending Adam and Eve out of the garden and preventing their return. They no longer had access to the tree of life; even so, the longing for the tree persists in us to this day (cf. Deut. 16:21; Rev. 22:2, 14, 19).

The cross of Jesus Christ has become our tree of life. Jesus, the Lamb of God, was lifted up and crucified upon a tree—a cross—so that "whoever believes in him may have eternal life" (John 3:15). Peter wrote, "[Christ] himself bore our sins in his body on the cross, so that, free from sins, we might live for righteousness" (1 Pet. 2:24). Therefore, the cross is the beloved sign and symbol of our new life, which is just the beginning.

Prayer:
Blessed Lord and giver of life:
We worship at the foot of our Savior's cross,
For here it was that he conquered sin and death.
Through Christ's death and resurrection, we now live,
And we will live to eat of the tree of life in the eternal city of God. Amen.

God's Covenant of Faith

First Reading: Gen. 17:1–8, 15:6
Poetry and Wisdom: Ps. 105:1–11
Second Reading: Luke 1:46–55, 67–75

"Abram believed the LORD; and the LORD reckoned it to him as righteousness." (Gen. 15:6)

——————————

Four hymns welcome the announcement and birth of Jesus in the Gospel of Luke: Mary's "Magnificat" (1:46–55), Zechariah's "Benedictus" (1:68–79), the angels' "Gloria" (2:14), and Simeon's "Nunc Dimittis" (2:29–32). The hymns of Mary and Zechariah announce the fulfillment of the covenant promise made to Father Abraham centuries earlier (cf. 1:55, 73).

God called Abram to leave the land of his forefathers and migrate to the land of Canaan. There he and his descendants would be blessed and become a great nation. According to the scriptures, Abram believed God's covenant promise and obeyed: "So Abram went, as the Lord had told him" (Gen. 12:1–4). At each stage of their tribal migration, Abram "built an altar to the Lord and invoked the name of the Lord" (12:7–8). God renewed his covenant promise with Abram four more times in the unfolding story (Gen. 13:14–18; 15:1–6, 18; 17:1–8; 22:17–18). Because of his responses of faith and obedience, God changed his name from Abram (Heb. "father / exalted ancestor") to Abraham (Heb. "father of a multitude"). He believed God's covenant promise—God's word—when there was no visible, concrete evidence to do so. "He believed the Lord; and the Lord reckoned it to him as righteousness" (Gen. 15:6).

The Lord God remembered and reaffirmed his covenant with Moses and Israel in Egypt and the Exodus (Exod. 2:24; 6:4f; 19:5), and the conditions remained the same: "*If* you obey my voice and keep my covenant, you shall be my treasured possession out of all the peoples. Indeed, the whole earth is mine, but you shall be for me a priestly kingdom and a holy nation" (Exod. 19:5). Those who believe God's promise, obey!

The cross proclaims God's reaffirmation of his covenant with the Jews and furthermore inclusively to the entire human race. It beckons everyone to respond to God's love and to enter into a new relationship with him. John writes, "To *ALL* who received [Jesus Christ], who believed in his name, he gave power to become children of God, who were born, not of blood or of the will of the flesh or of the will of man, but of God" (John 1:12–13). To this, John adds, "For God so loved the world that he gave his only Son, so that *everyone who believes* in him may not perish but may have eternal life" (John 3:16; cf. 3:36; 6:35; 12:44). That is the good news of the gospel and God's covenant promise in a nutshell. Our response— our faith and obedience—is critical.

The question for today and tomorrow is the same as that which Jesus asked his disciples, "Do you now believe?" (John 16:31). Yes, we believe and obey! For the response of the people of God through the ages remains the same. The words of the Old Testament prophet Habakkuk are repeated multiple times in the New Testament, "The righteous live by their faith" (2:4; cf. Rom. 1:17; Gal. 3:11; Heb. 10:38). As we learn in the ancient story of Abraham, it is God who takes the initiative and calls us to a new, living relationship with him. You have been renamed, "child of God," and included among the "righteous," the "saints of God."

9

Prayer:

Gracious Lord and faithful God:

We praise and bless your name for the covenant promise

Open to everyone who believes in your Son, Jesus Christ.

You are indeed God and Father of a great multitude that no one can count

From every nation, from all tribes and peoples and languages … including me. Amen.

Week 1.4—Saturday

Choose Life!

First Reading: Deut. 30:6–20; Josh. 24:1–2, 13–15
Poetry and Wisdom: Ps. 16:1–11
Second Reading: Luke 9:57–62; 14:25–35*

"If any want to become my followers, let them deny themselves and take up their cross daily and follow me." (Luke 9:23)

―――――――――――――

Choose life! That was the last word and exhortation of Moses to the people of Israel (Deut. 30:11–20). Likewise, Joshua appealed to his generation, "Choose this day whom you will serve ... but as for me and my household, we will serve the Lord" (Josh. 24:15). The choice has consequences: life and prosperity or death and adversity, blessings or curses (Deut. 30:15, 19). Therefore, choose to "love the Lord your God with all your heart and with all your soul, in order that you may live" (Deut. 30:6). And again Moses exhorts, "If you obey the commandments of the Lord your God that I am commanding you today, by loving the Lord your God, walking in his ways, and observing his commandments, decrees, and ordinances, then you shall live ... and the Lord your God will bless you" (Deut. 30:16).

Jesus called this the first and greatest commandment of all: "The first is, 'Hear, O Israel: the Lord our God, the Lord is one; you shall love the Lord your God with all your heart, and with all your soul, and with all your mind, and with all your strength.' The second is this, 'You shall love your neighbor as yourself.' There is no other commandment greater than these" (Mark 12:29–31). He adds, "Do this, and you will live" (Luke 10:28).

The gospels appeal for us to believe that Jesus is God's promised Messiah, the Christ, who was anticipated in the law and the prophets. The Evangelist John writes, "To all who received him, who believed in his name, he gave power to become children of God, who were born, not of blood or of the will of the flesh or of the will of man, but of God" (John 1:12f). Believing is a decision to love and follow Jesus—to live according to the will and ways of God. It is not an impulsive decision, nor is it a decision made with conditions or reservations.

Ponder and consider the consequences. Choose life and love God first and foremost above all else. That is what Jesus did, and for him it meant to obey the heavenly Father, even to suffer and die upon the cross. The decision to believe and follow Jesus Christ, the Son of God, is the theme of the gospels. John summarizes his purpose at end of the fourth gospel, writing, "... so that you may come to believe ... and that through believing you may have life in his name" (John 20:30f).

This new life is the gift of God. Moses promised that "the Lord your God will circumcise your heart" (Deut. 30:6). Through believing, we have become someone new, a new creation of God (1 Cor. 5:17). Jesus described it as being "born from above" or "born of the Spirit" (John 3:3–8). We are "saved" from the consequences of sin and death in this present life and for all eternity (cf. John 3:17). We are now disciples of Jesus, and we have entered into the kingdom and reign of God.

Prayer:
Blessed Lord and King of our lives:
Reign in us today without a rival,
For there is no other—no god of survival and pleasure,
No god of possessions and wealth, or god of success and popularity.
We choose life and love you above all else. Amen.

* Gospel parallels: Matt. 8:19–22; 10:37–38; 5:13; Mark 9:50.

A True Disciple

First Reading: Deut. 4:1–14
Poetry and Wisdom: Ps. 119:1–16
Second Reading: Matt. 5:17–20; 7:21–27[1]

"Not everyone who says to me, 'Lord, Lord,' will enter the kingdom of heaven, but only the one who does the will of my Father in heaven." (Matt. 7:21)

Jesus's disciples love and obey God's commandments! Jesus states this quite plainly in Matthew 5:17–20 in which he reaffirms the words of Moses declared centuries earlier in Deuteronomy 4:2. Therefore the commandments continue to be the core curriculum for all those who believe and follow Jesus Christ. After his resurrection, Jesus appeared to his disciples and commissioned them to "go ... and make disciples of all nations, baptizing them ... and *teaching them* to obey everything that I have commanded you" (Matt. 28:19f).

A true disciple *does* the will of the Lord our God by keeping the commandments. Moses stated that this shows the world the wisdom and discernment of the people of God. Our obedience reveals our profound love for Jesus Christ, who said, "If you love me, you will keep my commandments" (John 14:15; cf. 14:21–24; 15:10). They stand as a moral code for healthy and joyful living, and choosing to live by them reveals our wisdom and discernment to the world. Furthermore, we are commanded to teach them to our children and grandchildren (Deut. 4:9), so that they avoid the painful experiences and any abiding scars of a foolish life.

In the Sermon on the Mount, Jesus commanded his followers to "let your light shine before others, so that they may see your good works and give glory to your Father in heaven" (Matt. 5:16). Our confession that Jesus is Lord must be revealed in our daily conduct and the fruit of our lives. Jesus said, "Not everyone who says to me, 'Lord, Lord,' will enter the kingdom of heaven, but only the one who *does* the will of my Father in heaven" (Matt. 7:21). Jesus does not call his disciples to a confession of faith alone but also to a faithful, fruitful life of obedience. Jesus adds, "Everyone then who hears these words of mine and *acts* on them will be like a wise man who built his house on rock" (Matt. 7:24).

This is the rock and firm foundation on which we build our lives—*hearing* and *doing* the will of God. God will evaluate and judge us according to what we have done. That should not be a surprise to us. Listen to this familiar theme in the sayings of Jesus:

> "For whoever *does* the will of my Father in heaven is my brother and sister and mother" (Matt. 12:50; cf. Mark 3:35; Luke 8:21).
> "For the Son of Man is to come with his angels in the glory of his Father, and then he will repay everyone *for what has been done*" (Matt. 16:27).

Jesus's parables of judgment—the wise and foolish servant (Matt. 24:45–51), the ten virgins or bridesmaids (Matt. 25:1–13), the talents (Matt. 25:14–30), and the separation of the sheep from the goats (Matt. 25:31–46)—illustrate this theme quite boldly and clearly. In the final judgment, the people of all the nations will be gathered, identified, and separated before the Great Shepherd like sheep and goats according to what they have done or failed to do.

God will judge everyone according to what they have done, and a true disciple *does* the will and work of God.[2]

Prayer:

O God of righteousness and truth:

Since the creation of the world, your eternal power and divine nature

Have been openly and plainly revealed for all to see and understand.

More clearly, the law and the prophets and the words of Jesus

Call us to a life of faith, repentance, obedience, and wisdom. Amen.

[1] Gospel parallels: Luke 16:17; 6:46–49; 13:26–27.

[2] Cf. Isa. 59:18; Jer. 17:10; 31:30; Ezek. 24:14; 33:20; Hos. 12:2; Matt. 12:36f; Luke 12:48; John 5:29; Acts 26:20; Rom. 2:6; 2 Cor. 5:10; Eph. 2:10; James 2:14, 24; 1 Pet. 1:17; Jude 1:15; Rev. 20:12–13.

Section 2

The Ten Commandments

Aka. The Decalogue or The Ten Words

Exodus 20:1–21
(Cf. Deuteronomy 5:6–21)

Tablet 1 Love the Lord Your God	Tablet 2 Love Your Neighbor
³You shall have no other gods before me.	¹³You shall not murder.
⁴You shall not make for yourself an idol.	¹⁴You shall not commit adultery.
⁷You shall not make wrongful use of the name of the Lord your God.	¹⁵You shall not steal.
⁸Remember the Sabbath day, and keep it holy.	¹⁶You shall not bear false witness.
¹²Honor your father and your mother.	¹⁷You shall not covet.

The Ten Commandments

First Reading: Exod. 20:1–17
Poetry and Wisdom: Ps. 119:33–48
Second Reading: Matt. 19:16–23*

"When God finished speaking with Moses on Mount Sinai, he gave him the two tablets of the covenant, tablets of stone, written with the finger of God." (Exod. 31:18)

———

Jesus taught his disciples to pray, "Our Father in heaven, hallowed be your name. Your kingdom come. Your will be done, on earth as it is in heaven" (Matt. 6:9f). How do we know the will of God? Jesus invites us to return to Mount Sinai, as the basic will of God remains the same from the beginning for all humanity.

In the Synoptic Gospels, we read of a rich young man who came running to Jesus with the most important question anyone could ask: "Teacher, what good deed must I do to have eternal life? (Matt. 19:16; cf. Mark 10:17; Luke 18:18). Jesus answered, "You know the commandments" (Mark 10:19; Luke 18:20):

> You shall not murder.
> You shall not commit adultery.
> You shall not steal.
> You shall not bear false witness.
> Honor your father and mother.

17

These commandments are summarized in the second great commandment: "You shall love your neighbor as yourself" (Matt. 19:19; cf. 22:39; Lev.19:18).

The young man responded, "I have kept all these; what do I still lack?" (Matt. 19:20). At this point, Jesus changed the conversation by inference to the first tablet of the Ten Commandments or Decalogue received by Moses—specifically, to the preamble and the first commandment: "I am the Lord your God, who brought you out of the land of Egypt, out of the house of slavery; you shall have no other gods before me" (Exod. 20:2–3). The man knew the first commandment. Jesus simply said to him, "If you wish to be perfect, go, sell your possessions, and give the money to the poor, and you will have treasure in heaven; then come, follow me" (Matt. 19:21). Aha! The true love of the young man's heart had been exposed.

The young man's many possessions and his wealth had become his god. In the Sermon on the Mount, Jesus said, "Where your treasure is, there your heart will be also" (Matt. 6:21; Luke 12:34). Furthermore, he adds, "No one can serve two masters; for a slave will either hate the one and love the other, or be devoted to the one and despise the other. You cannot serve God and wealth" (Matt. 6:24; cf. Luke 16:13). The young man had chosen another god, his possessions.

The Ten Commandments are timeless, normative principles of law and behavior unknown in any other ancient law code— that is, these ten laws are peculiar to Israel alone. They are called apodictic laws, for they express an absolute standard for behavior, comprehensive and imperative in nature. Jesus said, "Do not think that I have come to abolish the law or the prophets ... For truly I tell you, until heaven and earth pass away, not one letter, not one stroke of a letter, will pass from the law until all is accomplished" (Matt. 5:17–18).

The story of the rich young ruler affirms the eternal nature of the law and that we must love the Lord our God supremely—more than any possession, person, or power. He will not permit a rival.

Prayer:

Dear Lord and author of the commandments:
Your will and wisdom are clearly revealed in these ten principles
Engraved on two tablets of stone and received on Mount Sinai.
May they be written on our hearts, so that we perpetually obey them,
Inspired by a supreme love for you and your Son, Jesus Christ. Amen.

* Gospel parallels: Mark 10:17–23; Luke 18:18–24.

Week 2.3—Tuesday

The First Commandment

First Reading: Exod. 20:1–3; Deut. 6:1–9
Poetry and Wisdom: Ps. 78:1–8
Second Reading: Mark 12:28–34[1]

"You shall have no other gods before me." (Exod. 20:3)

━━━━━━━━

The Bible does not argue for the existence of God. He is assumed to be—"In the beginning when God created the heavens and the earth ..." (Gen. 1:1). God is the creator, the intelligent designer, the source of all life, cosmic order, wisdom, and the moral law. The Ten Commandments (aka Decalogue—"the ten words," Exod. 34:28) are ten comprehensive, prohibitive statements that reveal the very nature and love of God for a peaceful, orderly, and prosperous people, culture, and society. They are the concise, living will of God for all times, people, and places—timeless, universal, moral laws.

Unlike the apodictic, moral prohibitions of the Ten Commandments, the Mosaic law also contains civil or case laws (e.g., Covenant Code, Exod. 20:22–23:33), which may be similar to other law codes in ancient cultures (e.g., Hammurabi). The religious or cultural laws (Leviticus, aka the Priests' Manual; esp., the Holiness Code, Lev. 17:1–26:46) apply specifically to the religious, purity, and ceremonial theocracy of Israel. At the council of Jerusalem in AD 49 (Acts 15:6–21; Gal. 2:1–10), the early Christian community and leadership determined that Gentiles or non-Jewish believers in Jesus the Messiah were not required to live according to the

Jewish laws (e.g., dietary, Sabbath, purification, and circumcision). Therefore, while the Old Testament case laws may provide wisdom and merit for a modern, orderly, civil society, the religious and civil laws were not included in the commandments of Jesus or endorsed as authoritative for Gentiles by the early church.

In the prologue to the Ten Commandments, God introduced himself: "I am the Lord your God, who brought you out of the land of Egypt, out of the house of slavery" (Exod. 20:2). He identified himself by two names—first as *Yahweh* (Lord, creator, life giver, covenant keeper, the eternal, loving "I am" [cf. Exod. 3:14]) and second as *'Elohim* (God, strong, powerful, the Almighty, the covenant enforcer [cf. Gen. 46:3]). The Lord God revealed himself to Israel, to the Egyptians, and to all humanity in the Exodus. He alone was the redeemer and liberator of Israel in their defining moment of history. Therefore the Lord God is supreme, and he alone is worthy of our love, obedience, and worship.

The first commandment prohibits polytheism and idolatry and commands the fear, love, and worship of the Lord God alone. The common recitation of the Shema in worship reaffirmed monotheism in Israel in succeeding generations: "Hear, O Israel: The Lord is our God, the Lord alone. You shall love the Lord your God with all your heart, and with all your soul, and with all your might" (Deut. 6:4f). The first commandment is the foundation on which the remaining nine build, and it is an essential theme throughout the Old Testament.[2]

For Jewish and Gentile believers in Jesus Christ, the prologue to the commandments has been enhanced and broadened. Whereas the Exodus of Israel remains a pivotal event, the death and resurrection of Jesus Christ was the Lord our God's supreme act of love and deliverance of all people who were held in the slavery and bondage of sin and death. Therefore, you shall have no other gods before him!

Prayer:
Ever loving Lord, my Redeemer and Savior from sin:
You, O Lord my God, are Lord alone; there is no other.
I love and worship you with all my heart,
And with all my soul, and with all my mind,
And with all my strength. Amen.

[1] Gospel parallels: Matt. 22:34–40; Luke 10:25–28.
[2] For example, Matt. 4:10; Luke 4:8; Exod. 22:20; Deut. 10:20; 13:4; Ps. 62; Isa. 37:20; 45:14, 21; Jer. 35:15; Dan. 3:29.

Week 2.4—Wednesday

The Second Commandment

First Reading: Exod. 20:4–6; Deut. 4:12
Poetry and Wisdom: Ps. 97:1–12
Second Reading: John 4:1–26

"You shall not make for yourself an idol." (Exod. 20:4)

———————

An idol is an image carved or sculpted from wood or stone, or formed in bronze or precious metal. The second commandment forbids both our creative activity and the worship of any physical representation of any deity. Thus the commandment prohibits the creation of any physical or material image of God himself, for he is spirit (John 4:24). He is the living God (Matt. 16:16). He cannot be limited to any one thing, time, or place. He cannot be boxed into a chapel or cathedral, nor can he be represented by any skilled image created by human hands. For this reason, the worship of Israel (Judaism) and Christianity is devoid of representations of God.

God has revealed himself in his word. In creation, "God said," and it came to be (Gen. 1:3 et al.). "God spoke all these words" of the commandments (Exod. 20:1). In these last days, God has revealed himself most clearly in Jesus Christ, his Son, the living Word of God (John 1:1f). The scriptures are revered as containing the word and revelation of God to all humankind, and we study them to know God more perfectly. God continues to speak to us in his Word.

The people of God have too often failed to obey the second commandment. Before Moses descended from Mount Sinai with the two engraved tablets, the Israelites persuaded Aaron the high priest to form a gold bull for them. They proclaimed a festive celebration dedicated to the worship of their precious, new symbol of their god with eating, drinking, dancing, and reveling (Exod. 32:1–6). If Moses had not interceded for Israel, God would have destroyed them in his anger.

Years later, when defeated by the Philistines, Israel concluded that if they carried the ark of the covenant into battle, God would be present with them, reverse their defeat, and give them victory (1 Sam. 4:1–9). Sadly, 30,000 Israelite soldiers died in the subsequent battle, and the Philistines captured the ark (1 Sam. 4:10f). The ark itself had become an idol rather than a box containing the Ten Commandments. Therefore, a cross, a crucifix, a Bible, an icon, or other religious artifact can become more than a reminder of God, becoming our god.

The Lord our God is a jealous God, and he will not tolerate a rival. Jesus reminded the Pharisees that they could not serve two masters, for they "will either hate the one and love the other, or be devoted to the one and despise the other. You cannot serve God and wealth" (Luke 16:13; Matt. 6:24). People, positions, powers, and possessions too frequently become the idols of our own making, displacing our love and worship of God.

If for no other reason, we are motivated to keep the second commandment, because our obedience will have excellent benefits for us now and for generations to come. If we disregard this commandment, the punishment will be experienced by our grandchildren and great-grandchildren (Exod. 20:5; 34:7; Num. 14:18ff). However, the benefits of our faithful worship of the Lord will extend to a thousand generations (Deut. 5:10; 7:9; Ps. 105:8; Lam. 3:22ff). The steadfast love and blessings of the Lord will come to us and to those who follow in future generations.

Prayer:

O holy and living Lord our God:

You alone are worthy of our worship and praise.

We are reminded of you in the wind, earthquake, and fire;

However, we hear you today in the sound of silence,

By the reading and meditation upon your word. Amen.

The Third Commandment

First Reading: Exod. 3:1–22; 20:7
Poetry and Wisdom: Ps. 113:1–9
Second Reading: Mark 3:20–35*

"You shall not make wrongful use of the name of the Lord your God." (Exod. 20:7; Deut. 5:11)

―――――――――

The God of Abraham, Isaac, and Jacob appeared to Moses at the burning bush on Mount Horeb (Exod. 3:1–12), for he had seen the misery and suffering of Israel in their slavery. He commissioned Moses to return to Egypt and free Israel from Pharaoh and their taskmasters. By what authority? On the authority of the God of their ancestors. What was his name? God said to Moses, "I am who I am." He said further, "Thus you shall say to the Israelites, 'I Am has sent me to you'" (Exod. 3:14). "This is my name forever, and this my title for all generations" (Exod. 3:15).

"I Am." The Hebrew name has four characters or letters [YHWH, aka Tetragrammaton], and, as an imperfect verb, it implies "beginning/past," "present," and "continues/future." Yahweh was, is, and will be. He is the unchanging, living One—the same yesterday, today, and forever (Heb. 13:8). The NIV and NRSV translate the divine name Yahweh as "the Lord" (cf. Exod. 3:15; 20:2, 7). Sometimes the KJV translated the Lord's name as "Jehovah" (cf. Exod. 6:3; Ps. 83:18), which is grammatically improper. Jesus asserted his own deity as the Son of God by frequently referring to himself as the "I am" (e.g., John 6:35; 8:12; 10:7, 11; 11:25; 14:6; 15:1; Rev. 1:8; et al.).

The Lord's name represents his nature, character, reputation, and his redeeming, saving love, witnessed supremely in the creation, the exodus and the cross of Jesus. The third commandment prohibits any wrongful or unworthy use of the divine name that defames, disrespects, tarnishes, or insults the holy character of God, thus damaging the Lord's reputation.

In the gospel, the scribes discredited and slandered the character of Jesus ascribing the work of God in the miracles to the activity and power of Beelzebul or Satan. This was blasphemy! For the miracles of Jesus were revealing the presence and power of the Holy Spirit among them. They were transgressing the third commandment, discrediting Jesus as a worker of evil—"having an unclean spirit" (Mark 3:22–30). Jesus sternly warned the scribes, "Whoever blasphemes against the Holy Spirit can never have forgiveness, but is guilty of an eternal sin" (Mark 3:29), which reaffirms the warning of the third commandment, "… the Lord will not acquit anyone who misuses his name" (Exod. 20:7).

Jesus taught his disciples to pray, "Our Father in heaven, hallowed be your name" (Matt. 6:9). God's name is holy and worthy of profound reverence and sacred awe. It is not to be used in an unworthy, disrespectful manner, which therefore prohibits false and trivial swearing, cursing, and incantations of evil (cf. Matt. 5:5:33–37; Lev. 24:15f). The true employment of the name of God exalts and recognizes his nature and character and is appropriately spoken in invocation, prayer, praise, and thanksgiving, which proceeds from a pure, believing heart.

My father reminded me that he had little earthly wealth to leave me, but he gave me a good name. I was blessed with a good family name—a good reputation in the rural Hoosier community. Likewise, when we say that we are children of God, do we take his name in vain and are we worthy of his family name? The third commandment safeguards the Lord's name and reputation.

Prayer:

Holy Yahweh and Father of our Lord Jesus Christ:
Your name is holy and worthy of our reverence and awe.
Master our tongues and purify our speech
From the careless, casual, and common use of your name
In coarse, vulgar cursing and unworthy repetition. Amen.

* Gospel parallels: Matt. 12:22–32; Luke 11:14–23; 12:10.

Week 2.6—Friday

The Fourth Commandment

First Reading: Gen. 2:1–3; Exod. 20:8–11; Deut. 5:12–15
Poetry and Wisdom: Ps. 84:1–12
Second Reading: Mark 2:23–28; 3:1:6*

"Remember the Sabbath day, and keep it holy." (Exod. 20:8)

───────

"Remember the Sabbath day" implies that Israel had prior knowledge and understanding of the supreme significance of the seventh day. Remember God's creative design from the beginning: "God rested on the seventh day from all the work that he had done. So God blessed the seventh day and hallowed it" (Gen. 2:1–3).

Remember you were slaves in Egypt, and the Lord brought you out of the house of slavery (Exod. 20:2). Remember the manna miraculously appeared in the wilderness for six days but not on the seventh, for the Sabbath "is a day of solemn rest, a holy Sabbath to the Lord" (Exod. 16:23). The Hebrew word *shabbat* means "to rest, to sit still, to cease from activity and work." Remember the Sabbath was built into the very structure of the universe for our benefit, the benefit of our families, of our employees, of those who provide for our needs, of our livestock and machinery, and of our neighbors. Remember this is the divine plan for a healthy, happy rhythm to life.

The Jews and Jesus himself understood the Sabbath as a reference to the seventh day—a day to rest from work and consecrated for the worship of God. Remember Jesus customarily worshipped in a synagogue on the Sabbath (Luke 4:16; 6:6; Mark 1:21). Even though the assembly for worship requires pastors and priests to lead their congregations, Jesus said that these religious leaders are not guilty of breaking the law of the Sabbath (Matt. 12:5; John 7:23). Jesus declared by word and example that it was a day for "doing good, to save lives" (cf. Mark 3:4), to heal (Luke 14:3; John 5:9; 9:14), to feed and water one's livestock (Luke 13:15), to rescue a person or an animal in distress or physical need (Luke 14:5), to harvest grain, prepare food, and eat (Mark 2:23), and to enjoy a feast with one's friends (Luke 14:1). It was not a day for fasting, extensive travel (Matt. 24:20), or burying the dead (Luke 23:56; Mark 16:1).

Jesus reaffirmed the divine purpose when he said, "The Sabbath was made for humankind, and not humankind for the Sabbath" (Mark 2:27). God created the Sabbath for our benefit. The Sabbath is the gift of God for the people of God—not as a legalistic burden hard to endure but as a blessing to those who obey his commandments (cf. Luke 11:46). Jesus reaffirms God's purpose for the Sabbath—for rest, relief, and refreshment (Exod. 23:12).

The death and resurrection of Jesus on Easter, the first day of the week, changed the Sabbath for all who believe and follow the Savior. Jesus appeared to his disciples five times on the first day of the week following his resurrection (Luke 24:13, 29, 36; John 20:11, 19, 26). Therefore the Lord's Day, the first day, became the new Sabbath and day for rest, relief, refreshment, and worship for Christians (cf. Acts 20:7; 1 Cor. 16:2; Rev. 1:10). The seventh-day Sabbath was converted or replaced by a new Sabbath, the Lord's Day, the first day of the week. Therefore, Christians keep the fourth commandment by observing the Lord's Day as a Sabbath and a sign of their identity and devotion to Jesus Christ.

Prayer:

Dear Lord of the Sabbath:

Teach us how to love and celebrate the holy day

Set apart from the other six for rest and relief from work.

Teach us how to live with a new healthy harmony,

Giving priority to worship, prayer, and spiritual refreshment. Amen.

*Gospel parallels: Matt. 12:1–14; Luke 6:1–11.

Week 2.7—Saturday

The Fifth Commandment

First Reading: Exod. 20:12; Lev. 19:1–3; Deut. 5:16
Poetry and Wisdom: Prov. 1:7–8; 10:1; 17:6; 20:20
Second Reading: Mark 7:1–23*

"Honor your father and your mother." (Exod. 20:12)

————————

Fathers and mothers are the representatives of God. As God is loved, respected, and honored, so too are one's parents. Thus, the fifth commandment belongs on the first tablet of the law and is associated with our love and obligations to God—reverence for his name and the keeping of the Sabbath (Lev. 19:3). When you love and honor your father and mother, you are showing love and honor to God.

The failure to honor one's parents was a serious violation of the law of God. In fact, if a child struck or cursed her/his father or mother, the penalty was the same as for murder (Exod. 21:12–17; Lev. 20:9). In Lev. 19:3, "honor" is replaced with "revere"—"You shall each revere your mother and father." Reverence is to be shown to one's parents in thought, word, and deed.

The fifth commandment contains a twofold promise: "… so that your days may be long in the land that the Lord your God is giving you" (Exod. 20:12). First, long life is promised to the one who honors her/his parents (cf. Ps. 37:28f). Second, the promise and benefit extends beyond the individual to the community, the nation, and the land. "Honor your father and your mother" lays a firm foundation for an orderly, peaceful, and prosperous society—a social network and safety net of family values.

The commandment protects elderly and infirm parents from abuse when they are no longer able to work and care for themselves. Hear the wisdom of the Proverbs: "Those who do violence to their father and chase away their mother are children who cause shame and bring reproach" (Prov. 19:26); "Listen to your father who begot you, and do not despise your mother when she is old" (Prov. 23:22). The psalmist's prayer to God may also be an appeal to one's children: "Do not cast me off in the time of old age; do not forsake me when my strength is spent" (Ps. 71:9). A barbarous and hardhearted people show no respect to the elderly and especially to the widow (cf. Deut. 28:50; Exod. 22:21).

Jesus closed a traditional loophole by which some were evading their responsibility to their father or mother. In Mark 7:1–23, the Pharisees and scribes were criticizing Jesus and his disciples for their failure to observe and practice the traditions of the elders, especially the rituals of purity—washing the hands, food, and eating utensils. These were human precepts and traditions that had become rigid rules of religious piety. Jesus severely condemns the lawyers, saying, "You abandon the commandment of God and hold to human tradition" (Mark 7:8).

According to their tradition, if a person pledged to give a gift or offering to God (Hebrew "Corban"), the vow could not be broken, changed, or withdrawn, thereby redeeming the gift for the benefit of one's parents who were in need (cf. Lev. 27:1–34). The offering could be money, land, an animal, a period of religious discipline, or even a lifetime in holy service, such as entering the holy orders of the priesthood or the pastoral ministry. Jesus counters that such noble vows do not excuse anyone from the commandment to honor and care for one's father or mother (Mark 7:9–13). Human traditions and vows do not nullify the fifth commandment.

Prayer:
Our Father who is in heaven:
Thank you for my earthly father and mother
Who gave me birth and nursed and nurtured me in my youth,
Teaching me by word and example to fear and love the Lord
In my quest for knowledge, wisdom, and an honorable life. Amen.

* Gospel parallel: Matt. 15:1–20.

Week 3.1—Sunday

The Sixth Commandment

First Reading: Exod. 20:13; 21:12–14; Lev. 19:15–18;
                        Num. 35:16–30
Poetry and Wisdom: Ps. 69:1–20
Second Reading: Matt. 5:17–26*

"You shall not murder." (Exod. 20:13)

"You shall not murder" (Exod. 20:13) includes the intentional and unintentional, premeditated and accidental, willful and unwillful taking the life of another human being. Ancient and modern law distinguishes between murder (premeditation, malice, and intention) and involuntary manslaughter (without motive, enmity, or intent). The latter is sometimes called "an act of God" (Exod. 21:13). Mosaic law stipulated that the murderer must be put to death. However, justice required total impartiality of judgment—without bias for or against the poor or powerful (Lev. 19:15). Justice must be socially and culturally blind and provided by the community (Num. 35:24f). Furthermore, a death sentence required the evidence of two or more witnesses (Num. 35:30). The fallibility of determining true, impartial justice in modern Western society has practically eliminated capital punishment.

Jesus corroborates the sixth commandment in the first of six "antitheses" in the Sermon on the Mount (Matt. 5:21–48). The antitheses are corrective clarifications of the common traditional interpretations. While affirming the righteous nature of the original law, Jesus appeals for a new awareness of the grand, heavenly intention of God. He restates the original law: "You have heard that it was said to those of ancient times, 'You shall not murder'; and 'whoever murders shall be liable to judgment'" (Matt. 5:21). Jesus then asserts that the spirit of the law likewise prohibits acts of verbal abuse and bullying. Anger, insults, and curses are also forms of murder *with the tongue*. Jesus warned his followers that "on the day of judgment you will have to give an account for every careless word you utter; for by your words you will be justified, and by your words you will be condemned" (Matt. 12:36f). True, these verbal attacks may be considered lesser transgressions than taking a life; however, they are assaults upon the character, reputation, and self-esteem of another person. As the ancient Chinese proverb says, "The tongue, like a sharp knife, kills without drawing blood." For such emotional forms of hatred and abuse, there is likewise responsibility and liability.

Jesus creates a crescendo concerning murder with the tongue (i.e., anger > insults > curses) and a similar warning of increasing liability. He alludes to three courts of justice: the community, the council, and the Creator. First, words spoken in anger tarnish and corrode the reputation of the offender within the community. Second, an insult attacks the character and honor of another, and the hurtful deed may result in official proceedings for libel or slander in a civil court of law. The third example of murder with the tongue calls for the most serious judgment and condemnation of the offender. "If you say, 'You fool,' you will be liable to the hell of fire" (Matt. 5:22). In the context of scripture, this is a curse and a pronouncement of eternal judgment upon oneself. The offender is admonished to "come to terms quickly with your accuser" and avoid the disgrace, shame, and a possible prison sentence before a human judge and the eternal judge as well.

Those who follow Jesus are to live by the spirit of the law. The sixth commandment, therefore, prohibits murder with the tongue. Furthermore, Jesus makes *repentance, restitution,* and *reconciliation* with one's neighbor the prerequisite condition and preparation for the three Rs in the worship of the living God. The law of love requires the healing of hurts and unites the community in true righteousness before our holy Lord.

Prayer:

Dear Lord and Judge of our thoughts, words, and deeds:

Your Son, our Savior, has reminded us of the abiding nature of your law,

Translating the meaning of murder engraved on the tablet of stone

To include anger, insults, and curses that assault the character and lives of others.

Forgive my hurtful words and write this commandment upon the flesh of my heart. Amen.

* Gospel parallels: Mark 13:31; Luke 12:57–59; 16:17; 21:33.

Week 3.2—Monday

The Seventh Commandment

First Reading: Exod. 20:14; Lev. 20:10–16
Poetry and Wisdom: Prov. 6:20–35
Second Reading: Matt. 5:27–37

"You shall not commit adultery." (Exod. 20:14)

———————

The seventh commandment, "You shall not commit adultery" (Ex. 20:14), forbids sexual relations between a married (or engaged) person and anyone other than one's wife or husband. Furthermore, the law stipulated that both the woman and the man who were proven guilty of such sexual immorality shall be put to death by stoning and thus purged from among the people of Israel (Deut. 22:22–24). In the Gospel of John 8:2–11, the scribes and the Pharisees brought a woman to Jesus who had been caught in the very act of adultery, and they cited the commandment that she should be stoned. Jesus responded, after writing in the dust of the ground, "Let anyone among you who is without sin be the first to throw a stone at her" (John 8:7). Thereafter the crowd dispersed, beginning with the elders.

Thus, Jesus abolished stoning! Why? There was no one without sin and qualified to cast a stone at the adulterer or the adulteress. Stoning was a cruel, excessively harsh, and barbaric punishment. On the other hand, the seventh commandment sanctifies and preserves marriage between a man and a woman, and the ancient punishment for its violation highlights the serious nature of this transgression in the eyes of God.

In the Sermon on the Mount, Jesus confirmed the law's prohibition against committing adultery (Matt. 5:27). Then he corrects and clarifies the warning of the commandment, highlighting the seemingly "innocent" seed and beginning of a potential breach: "But I say to you that everyone who looks at a woman [man] with lust has already committed adultery with her [him] in his [her] heart" (Matt. 5:28–30).

Adultery has its roots in a lustful look and a lustful touch. What may seem like an excusable, rather innocent beginning must be radically and abruptly stopped or it may grow and mature into an adulterous affair. Did Jesus command his followers who are lured by sexual temptations to literally tear out the eye or cut off the hand? No, absolutely not! Self-mutilation is not endorsed in any way. However, Jesus passionately warns his followers with this radical figure of speech. Lust can lead to the transgression of God's law with serious earthly and eternal consequences.

When does looking, touching, or walking toward a thing or person with regard to sex become a forbidden lust or adultery in one's imagination? Temptations originate with the natural, God-given desires, and like the tongue, they must be self-disciplined. These natural desires are like wild horses, which must be tamed, bridled, and mastered. Just as the tongue is necessary for tasting, swallowing, and speaking, it can also be used as an instrument for gossip and the destruction of others. Sexual desire is God's gift as well, and it creates a desire for another person.

We live in a sex-saturated society. Unless a person is blind and deaf, it is impossible to avoid seeing and hearing multiplied sexual references and innuendos in the media, on the street, and in the common vulgar language of the day. It is everywhere! Seeing or hearing these sexual enticements may create a temptation. However, the temptation itself is not sin.

James, the first bishop of the church in Jerusalem, alerted his readers to anticipate temptations and trials as long as they lived. When the temptation is welcomed and allowed to linger in one's thoughts, sin is at the very door. "When that desire has conceived, it gives birth to sin" (James 1:15). When the seed is welcomed and watered in one's thoughts, it will sprout and begin to grow. The temptation has become lust.

Therefore, Jesus addressed the issue of pornography, masturbation, sex toys, and immodest attire. The burden of responsibility, however, lies with the lustful perpetrator—the one who looks, touches, and/or visits such places to indulge in sexual fantasies, flirtations, and freedom from shame. The venue may be public or private. Whatever the source, Jesus warns that radical action is required.

Prayer (*Collect for Purity*):
Almighty God
 to whom all hearts are open,
 all desires known,
 and from whom no secrets are hid:
Cleanse the thoughts of our hearts
 by the inspiration of your Holy Spirit
 that we may perfectly love you
 and worthily magnify your holy name,
Through Jesus Christ our Lord. Amen.

* Gospel parallels: Matt. 19:3–9, 18; Mark 10:2–12, 19; Luke 16:18; 18:20; John 8:2–11.

The Eighth Commandment

First Reading: Exod. 20:15; 22:1–15
Poetry and Wisdom: Prov. 30:1–9
Second Reading: Luke 3:1–14*

"You shall not steal." (Exod. 20:15)

The eighth commandment, "You shall not steal," prohibits any act of taking for oneself or causing the loss of something of value belonging to another. As observed in the Old Testament readings, stealing may include kidnapping a person (Exod. 21:16), taking an ox or a sheep belonging to another (Exod. 22:1), allowing or causing the injury, loss, or destruction of another person's property (Exod. 22:5–6), or the careless failure to provide safekeeping for borrowed or loaned property in one's possession (Exod. 22:15).

Stealing has numerous modern synonyms and forms: theft, robbery, burglary, larceny, cheating, fleecing, embezzling, defrauding, extorting, scamming, conning, deceiving, swindling, counterfeit, rip-off, Ponzi scheme, and more. John the Baptist called his generation to repentance for the forgiveness of sins and in preparation for the coming of the salvation of God through Jesus Christ. John exhorted his listeners to "bear fruits worthy of repentance" (Luke 3:8).

> The crowds asked him, "What then should we do?
> In reply he said to them, "Whoever has two coats

> must share with anyone who has none; and whoever has food must do likewise." Even tax collectors came to be baptized, and they asked him, "Teacher, what should we do?" He said to them, "Collect no more than the amount prescribed for you." Soldiers also asked him, "And we, what should we do?" He said to them, "Do not extort money from anyone by threats or false accusation, and be satisfied with your wages." (Luke 3:12–14)

The universal evidence of repentance is generosity and sharing what one has with the poor, hungry, and the less fortunate (cf. Matt. 25:31–40). The Lord calls us to be a people of the "open hand" rather than the "closed fist." Selfishness and blindness to the needs of others may be a transgression of the eighth commandment, for stealing may be a sin of omission as well as the commission of a theft.

Clearly, John the Baptist understood stealing to be related to greed, dishonesty, cheating, extortion, and blackmail. It may be an employer or a corporation holding back wages, overtime pay, or benefits due to a worker. Exorbitant salaries and benefits paid to upper management and corporate officers is a form of stealing from other employees and shareholders. It may be a religious organization fleecing their devotees. This was the egregious transgression of the temple moneychangers eliciting Jesus's condemnation: "Is it not written, 'My house shall be called a house of prayer for all the nations'? But you have made it a den of robbers" (Mark 11:17). Entrance into God's house of prayer and salvation itself must never be abused with demands for money.

Plagiarism and the misuse of copyrighted materials as one's own and/or without giving credit to the original author or source is a form of stealing. An addiction to substances (e.g., alcohol, cocaine, et al.) and compulsive, pleasurable activities (e.g., gambling, sex, shopping, et al.) that interfere with and destroy one's own health, work, relationships, and responsibilities to spouse, family, employer, and God are forms of stealing.

The apostle Paul declared, "Thieves must give up stealing; rather let them labor and work honestly with their own hands, so as to have something to share with the needy" (Eph. 4:28). The eighteenth-century churchman John Wesley exhorted everyone to "gain all you can by honest industry" and gave three plain rules for the management of money according to God's design: "Gain all you can ... Save all you can ... [and] Give all you can" (Sermon 50: "The Use of Money").

Prayer:
Blessed Lord of light, life, and love:
Your law is holy and just and good, for it illuminates what is right and wrong.
Through the law comes the knowledge of sin and our great need of forgiveness and salvation.
Your law teaches us the importance of storing up for ourselves treasures in heaven,
Where neither moth nor rust consumes and where thieves do not break in and steal. Amen.

* Gospel parallels: Matt. 3:1–10; Mark 1:1–6.

Week 3.4—Wednesday

The Ninth Commandment

First Reading: Exod. 20:16; 23:1–3; Deut. 19:15–21
Poetry and Wisdom: Ps. 52:1–9
Second Reading: Matt. 5:33–37

"You shall not bear false witness." (Exod. 20:16)

———————————

The ninth commandment, "You shall not bear false witness" (Exod. 20:16), prohibits giving a false or unfounded testimony in a court of law by which the reputation, life, marriage, or property of another person may be harmed or endangered. To protect a possible victim from a malicious accuser, the law prescribed that no one is to be condemned on the basis of one witness (Deut. 19:15). If a witness has been found guilty of swearing falsely in a court of law, the perjurer shall be punished with the punishment he/she wished to inflict on the one falsely accused (Deut. 19:18f).

In the Sermon on the Mount, Jesus affirms the ninth commandment in the fourth antithesis, and he appears to conflate the commandment with a phrase from Numbers 30:2—"You shall not swear falsely, but carry out the vows you have made to the Lord" (Matt. 5:33). Since the Lord God is all-knowing, all-seeing, and all-powerful, it is common to call upon God as witness and enforcer of the vows we make: "As God is my witness, I will do as I say." Therefore, Jesus connects the ninth commandment with the third: "You shall not make wrongful use of the name of the Lord your God" (Ex. 20:7). It would be a grave transgression to swear falsely while calling upon God to certify the intent and truth of one's words and vow.

The scribes and Pharisees understood and taught the legal letter of the law; however, they failed to understand, teach, and practice the spirit of the ninth commandment. Therefore, Jesus corrects the popular, common understanding:

> But I say to you, Do not swear at all, either by heaven, for it is the throne of God, or by the earth, for it is his footstool, or by Jerusalem, for it is the city of the great King. And do not swear by your head, for you cannot make one hair white or black. Let your word be 'Yes, Yes' or 'No, No'; anything more than this comes from the evil one." (Matt. 5:34–37; cf. Matt. 23:16–22; James 5:12)

Jesus calls his followers to understand, teach, and practice the spirit of the Torah—always tell the truth and fulfill what you promise. It should not be necessary to place one's hand on a Bible or to swear on a godly mother or father's grave for one to tell the truth. Jesus is calling his disciples to a higher standard of integrity, honesty, and truthfulness.

Outwardly, the scribes and Pharisees cultivated a reputation of righteousness and holy living—that is, observing the Sabbath; washing their hands, cups, pots, and kettles; praying conspicuously in public; fasting twice a week, and so on. Jesus harshly condemned this guild of lawyers and their kin, calling them "blind guides," "hypocrites," "snakes," and "vipers" (Matt. 23:13–36). Why? They were hypocrites and false witnesses of the righteousness of God.

Lying, dishonesty, gossip, flattery, and exaggeration—anything that deviates from the truth—is a false witness. The people of God are to be critical thinkers, careful defenders, and loving promoters of the truth, protecting the character and reputation of God and others. By such, we fulfill the law of love.

Prayer:
God of justice, judgment, mercy, and love:
Your word is a lamp to my feet and a light to my path.
Your spirit purifies my heart and helps me bridle my tongue.
But still I have sinned many times in thought, word, and witness.
Have mercy, O Lord, and forgive my careless words that tarnish the
truth. Amen.

The Tenth Commandment

First Reading: Exod. 20:17
Poetry and Wisdom: Ps. 112:1–10; Prov. 21:26
Second Reading: Matt. 16:24–26*

"You shall not covet." (Exod. 20:17)

The tenth commandment, "You shall not covet" (Exod. 20:17), goes to the desires of the heart and the secret thoughts stirring in the mind. Jesus said, "What comes out of the mouth proceeds from the heart, and this is what defiles. For out of the heart come *evil intentions*," and then he lists the evil deeds and transgressions condemned in commandments six through nine, "murder, adultery, fornication, theft, false witness, slander" (Matt. 15:18). Coveting is that inner wish or craving for the abilities, attributes, possessions, wealth, or power of another person. It may begin with seemingly harmless thoughts and fantasies about what might be, "If only I had what belongs to another." The sin germinates in the form of envy, jealousy, greed, and lust.

Cain became angry and jealous of his brother Abel, and the Lord asked, "If you do well, will you not be accepted? And if you do not do well, sin is lurking at the door; its desire is for you, but you must master it" (Gen. 4:7). He coveted what Abel enjoyed before God, and he killed him (Gen. 4:8). The patriarch Jacob coveted the birthright inheritance rightfully belonging to his elder brother Esau. Therefore he conspired against Esau, deceived his father Isaac, and lied, cheating his brother of the prized blessing (Gen. 25:29–34; 27:1–45). King David had many concubines and wives (1 Sam. 5:13), but when he saw the very beautiful wife of his neighbor Uriah the Hittite, he had to have one more (i.e., Bethsheba) for himself (2 Sam. 11:1–5). When he learned that Bethsheba was pregnant with his child, David plotted the death of Uriah and took Bethsheba for his wife (2 Sam. 11:27). The stories of coveting are sadly quite numerous throughout history.

Coveting is a selfish and arrogant sin of the heart. It begins with a seemingly innocent God-given, natural desire that ensnares the thoughts, germinating, fantasizing, and plotting an evil fulfillment in the mind. James, the first bishop of Jerusalem, describes the deceptive, progressive nature of covetousness: "One is tempted by one's own desire, being lured and enticed by it; then, when that desire has conceived, it gives birth to sin, and that sin, when it is fully grown, gives birth to death. Do not be deceived, my beloved" (James 1:14–16). Our desires are like wild horses, and they must be mastered, harnessed, and disciplined for good and in harmony with the will of God.

What are the objects of one's coveting or quest? The neighbor's house, wife/husband, possessions, wealth, status, or anything that belongs to the neighbor, coworker, friend, or acquaintance. The list is all-inclusive, ruling out any ambiguity as to the extent of the neighbor's property. Coveting is the inward and often unrecognized cause of unhappiness, depression, moodiness, pessimism, strife, conflict, quarrels, dissensions, drunkenness, divorce, and criticism of others (cf. James 4:1–2). By contrast, those in whom the Spirit of God dwells are characterized by love, joy, peace, patience, kindness, generosity, faithfulness, gentleness, and self-control (cf. Gal. 5:22f).

Jesus warned his disciple about the covetous evil eye or green-eyed monster: "Take care! Be on your guard against all kinds of greed; for one's life does not consist in the abundance of possessions" (Luke 12:15).

Prayer:

O Lord, your commandments are holy, just, and good.

But now I know what is meant by, "You shall not covet!"

The covetous secrets of my heart and thoughts of my mind are exposed;

Envy, jealousy, greed, and lust have too frequently found a welcome,

Crowding out love, joy, peace, and contentment.

Deliver me, O God—cleanse my heart and master my thoughts—

Grant me true freedom and a victorious life through Jesus Christ our Lord. Amen.

* Gospel parallels: Mark 8:34–37; Luke 9:23–25.

Week 3.6—Friday

The Great Commandments

First Reading: Deut. 6:1–9; 10:12–13; 11:1; Lev. 19:11–18
Poetry and Wisdom: Ps. 1:1–6
Second Reading: Mark 12:28–34*

"You shall love the Lord your God with all your heart, and with all your soul, and with all your strength, and with all your mind; and your neighbor as yourself." (Luke 10:27)

God's love for all humanity is never in question. His love is not affected by emotions or doubts, as is our human love for him and others. "His steadfast love endures forever!" (Ps. 136).

Although Israel is the primary focus of God's love in the Old Testament, the divine passion and purpose is for Israel—as a nation and later in the Diaspora—to be a witness of God's love and redemption to the nations of the world (cf. Gen. 17:4; Lev. 18:24; Deut. 4:5–8; Isa. 2:2f; Jer. 31:10). In John 3:16, Jesus reaffirms God's love for the world. This is a universal and inclusive theme of the scriptures. There is no distinction of gender, race, ethnicity, language, culture, social status, or time in human history (cf. Rom. 8:38–39). God's "steadfast love" for you and me endures forever (cf. Ps. 107 and 136). Love is the primary attribute and defining nature of God (1 Jn. 4:8, 17), and nothing can separate us from God's pursuing and redeeming love.

On the other hand, the human response in the God-man relationship is flawed and fickle. The wily enemy of our immortal souls raises doubts, "Did God say …? Really?" (cf. Gen. 3:1). And we begin to question what we understand to be God's word and will. Is the proof of our love for God inseparably linked to his commandments? Yes! Jesus said, "If you love me, you will keep my commandments" (John 14:15; cf. 14:21; 15:10). If we love God, we keep his commandments. Yes, all of them! Our ethical behavior and conduct is the proof and witness of our love for God and neighbor.

God gave the law to Moses for the benefit of all his beloved people. The first five remind us that the Lord our God is God alone. He tolerates no rival. He is our creator and redeemer, and he cannot be represented by any earthly form, as he is spirit. His name is holy, and the Sabbath is a sacred day set aside for our rest from labor and for divine worship. Fathers and mothers are God's representatives and teachers by word and example of his law to their children and grandchildren. Jesus summarized these five commandments in the first great commandment: "You shall love the Lord your God with all your heart, and with all your soul, and with all your mind, and with all your strength" (Mark 12:30).

Engraved on the second stone tablet of the law were commandments six through ten. In these five commandments, God highly values human life, marriage, property, truthfulness, and disciplined desires. Six, seven, and eight prohibit the deeds of murder, adultery, and stealing. Nine prohibits false accusations against one's neighbor. The tenth commandment prohibits thoughts and craving to obtain the property of another. Jesus summarized them in the second great commandment: "You shall love your neighbor as yourself" (Mark 12:31).

These two great commandments—to love God and neighbor—summarize all God's law and the gospel. Love is both the nature of God and the essential character of his people.

Prayer:
Dear Jesus Christ, Lord of steadfast love:

51

You have modeled and mandated that your followers love, as our
Father in heaven loves the world and all people.

We strive to live a life of perfect love for God and neighbor, but we
fall woefully short of the cherished prize.

Have mercy upon us this day and forgive us of all our sins. Amen.

* Gospel parallels: Matt. 22:34–40; Luke 10:25–28.

Section 3

THE CANON OF THE CHRISTIAN FAITH

Canon—a measuring reed, ruler, scale or standard by which the literature is evaluated and determined worthy and authoritative for preservation and proclamation of divine truth.

The Canon of the Hebrew Bible or Old Testament (Thirty-Nine Books)*

The Law or Torah: Genesis, Exodus, Leviticus, Numbers, Deuteronomy

The Historical Books: Joshua, Judges, Ruth, 1 and 2 Samuel, 1 and 2 Kings, 1 and 2 Chronicles, Ezra, Nehemiah, Esther

Poetry and Wisdom: Job, Psalms, Proverbs, Ecclesiastes, Song of Solomon

The Prophetic Books: Isaiah, Jeremiah, Lamentations, Ezekiel, Daniel, Hosea, Joel, Amos, Obadiah, Jonah, Micah, Nahum, Habakkuk, Zephaniah, Haggai, Zechariah, Malachi

*Roman Catholic canon adds seven books: Tobit, Judith, Wisdom of Solomon, Ecclesiasticus (aka Sirach), Baruch, 1 and 2 Maccabees.

The Canon of the New Testament (Twenty-Seven Books)

Gospels: Matthew, Mark, Luke, and John

History of the Church: The Acts of the Apostles

Pauline Letters or Epistles: Romans, 1 and 2 Corinthians, Galatians, Ephesians, Philippians, Colossians, 1 and 2 Thessalonians, 1 and 2 Timothy, Titus, and Philemon

General Letters or Epistles: Hebrews, James, 1 and 2 Peter, 1, 2, and 3 John, and Jude

Prophecy: Revelation

The Truth of God

First Reading: Deut. 8:1–10
Poetry and Wisdom: Prov. 2:1–11; 3:13–18
Second Reading: John 18:33–38; 19:16–22

"Pilate asked Jesus, 'What is truth?'" (John 18:38)

———————————

The religious leaders charged Jesus with treason, and they clamored for his death by crucifixion. They said that he claimed to be the king of a new kingdom. Therefore, Pilate asked Jesus directly, "Are you the King of the Jews?" (John 18:33). Jesus responded, "My kingdom is not from this world" (John 18:36). "So you are a king?" With this Jesus agrees; however, his kingdom is not earthly, territorial, physical, or temporal. His kingdom transcends and exists beyond the world of sensory experiences. Jesus summarized his earthly mission, saying, "I came into the world, to testify to the truth. Everyone who belongs to the truth listens to my voice" (John 18:37). One wonders how much Pilate understood Jesus's explanation, for he then asked, "What is truth?" (John 18:38).

Pilate's profound question is also our quest. How do we determine what is true or the truth? Information technology provides us access to an infinite wealth of facts, fiction, and diverse opinions. It is a major challenge to learn and understand the facts and the truth from so much that is false in the rapidly expanding world of information, science, medicine, economics, politics, and so on. Furthermore, how do we, like Pilate, bridge the gap between the earthly and the heavenly, the physical and the spiritual realm of truth? How can we know and understand God's will and God's truth?

Experience: Jesus revealed his divine nature by doing deeds of power, wonders, and signs (cf. Acts 2:22). The crowds were amazed by his miracles, and many believed that he was indeed the Son of God (cf. John 2:23). Nicodemus is one such example. He came to Jesus and confessed, "Rabbi, we know that you are a teacher who has come from God; for no one can do these signs that you do apart from the presence of God" (John 3:2). He wanted to know more because of what he had seen and heard with his own eyes and ears.

Reason: Jesus's many sayings and parables tell a familiar earthly proverb, figure of speech, or story with a similar, parallel heavenly or kingdom lesson. Jesus attracted great crowds because he spoke with authority in a fresh style relevant to his listeners' daily experiences. Sometimes he was provocative and controversial. His listeners were captivated by the common life experiences or mental pictures, and they were forced to think and ponder the moral and spiritual truth. Jesus made his listeners think. Although he invited everyone to believe and become his disciple, Jesus also warned his listeners to first count the cost (Luke 9:58; 14:28).

Tradition: The people of Israel experienced the exodus from the slavery and suffering of Egypt. They wandered in the wilderness for forty years. God fed them with manna and quail (Exod. 16:13, 35) and quenched their thirst at his oases (Exod. 15:25; Num. 20:11). The exodus experience was God's means of teaching them to believe and trust him as the Lord their God (Deut. 8:1–10). The traditional Passover observance became their national, yearly festival of remembrance, teaching their children and generations to this day this valuable truth. Traditions preserve and serve to pass on lessons learned in ages past. The Christian traditions of observing the sacrament of the Lord's Supper, reciting the Lord's Prayer, and confessing our faith in the historic creeds continue to teach us and our children the grand truths of God.

Scripture: The fourth means by which we discover and know the will and truth of God is through the scriptures. Jesus countered the temptations of Satan (Luke 4:1–13) by saying, "It is written ..." followed by quotations from the law (Deut. 8:3; 6:3, 16). He corrected many Jewish traditions with the authority of the scriptures (e.g., Mark 11:17; 12:24). For Jesus and his first-century followers, the scriptures included the law, the prophets, and the psalms (i.e., the Hebrew Bible or Old Testament) (Luke 24:44). This will be the theme of the next devotional meditation.

Jesus invites his followers to an adventure of faith and discovery, to think critically, and thus to understand the nature of his kingdom. We test and know the truth by means of experience, reason, tradition, and scripture. Like Pilate, we are on a quest to know the truth, especially God's truth.

Prayer:
Holy Father, we bow and worship you in spirit and truth.
We live in a complex and challenging world
Of experience, reason, tradition, and scripture.
Grant to us discerning hearts and minds in our quest
To critically and correctly understand your kingdom and truth.
    Amen.

The Word of God: Old Testament

First Reading: Deut. 4:1–8
Poetry and Wisdom: Ps. 33:1–12
Second Reading: Luke 16:16–31

"If they do not listen to Moses and the prophets, neither will they be convinced even if someone rises from the dead." (Luke 16:31)

———————

In the quest to know the truth and will of God, there are four means by which we weigh the evidence and live by faith: experience, reason, tradition, and scripture.* All four are vital to a dynamic, living faith, but which one of the four do we consider to be the highest authority? Is our answer always the same?

Some are on a quest to experience the presence of God on a mountain, by the sea, in a garden, through prayer, or in worship with the people of God. Others ask what they consider to be the most important question, "Is it reasonable?" For them, faith must be supported by factual evidence and logical arguments. Thus, faith and science are reconcilable. Still others more highly value the traditions of faith—the sacraments, orderly worship, private and public prayers, generosity to the Lord's work and to the poor, fasting, pilgrimage, and the public reading of scripture. Of the four tests of truth, Jesus consistently quotes what is written in the scriptures as the highest authority over all. In his post-resurrection appearance to the apostles, Jesus said, "Everything written about me in the law of Moses, the prophets, and the psalms must be fulfilled" (Luke 24:44).

"The law, the prophets, and the psalms" refers to the three divisions of the Hebrew Bible, aka the Old Testament (OT). The thirty-nine books of the OT expressed the authoritative word of God to Jesus and his early followers. Soon Jesus's sayings, life, and teaching became authoritative for the early disciples, as they were treasured and passed on orally. Then in time they were collected, arranged, and written into the gospel narratives familiar to us. However, Jesus stated that all that was necessary for faith and salvation was found in the words of the OT—"If they do not listen to Moses and the prophets, neither will they be convinced even if someone rises from the dead" (Luke 16:31).

The books of the law and the prophets were written mostly in ancient Hebrew on sheets of papyrus or parchment and rolled into scrolls. The individual books were copied manually, collected and preserved in a cabinet in the community synagogues and in the temple. By the third century BC, many of the Jews were living scattered throughout the Hellenistic Roman Empire, and Greek was their first language. Therefore the scriptures were translated into a Greek version known as the Septuagint (LXX). This Greek version of the OT is of special interest. First, the apostles and early Christian writers quoted the scriptures from both the Hebrew and the Greek versions. Second, the LXX included the Apocrypha (i.e., as many as fourteen or fifteen additional books or portions of books). While the Catholic OT canon includes Tobit, Judith, Wisdom of Solomon, Ecclesiasticus (aka Sirach), Baruch, and 1 and 2 Maccabees found in the LXX, the Protestant OT canon limits the books to those found in the Hebrew or Palestinian canon list of scriptures.

By whom and how were the thirty-nine books selected to be included in the Old Testament? Over centuries of time, a canon, a standard or a rule of measurement, became accepted by which the many religious writings were evaluated, and chosen or rejected as worthy. The official canon list was ultimately fixed by rabbinical Judaism at the Council of Jamnia (ca. AD 90). In brief, those OT books worthy of inclusion in the sacred writings were chosen by five criteria: content (consistent with the Torah), prophetic inspiration

(God speaks to the worshiper/listener/reader), date (authentic prophecy ceased after Daniel), confessional (has a worthy function in worship), and Hebrew character (esp. excluding Christian literature). The popularity of the life and teaching of Jesus, the appearance of the gospels, and the flourishing Christian literature of the first century motivated their official decision. Therefore, in harmony with the Hebrew canon, the Protestant Old Testament canon includes the following thirty-nine books of scripture:

The Law or Torah: Genesis, Exodus, Leviticus, Numbers, Deuteronomy
The Historical Books: Joshua, Judges, Ruth, 1 and 2 Samuel, 1 and 2 Kings, 1 and 2 Chronicles, Ezra, Nehemiah, Esther
Poetry and Wisdom: Job, Psalms, Proverbs, Ecclesiastes, Song of Solomon
The Prophetic Books: Isaiah, Jeremiah, Lamentations, Ezekiel, Daniel, Hosea, Joel, Amos, Obadiah, Jonah, Micah, Nahum, Habakkuk, Zephaniah, Haggai, Zechariah, Malachi

Prayer (Psalm 25:4–7):
Make me to know your ways, O Lord;
　　teach me your paths.
Lead me in your truth, and teach me,
　　for you are the God of my salvation;
　　for you I wait all day long.
Be mindful of your mercy, O Lord,
　　and of your steadfast love,
　　for they have been from of old.
Do not remember the sins of my youth
　　or my transgressions;
According to your steadfast love remember me,
　　for your goodness' sake, O Lord! Amen.

---

* This four–way test is sometimes called the Wesleyan Quadrilateral.

The Word of God: New Testament

First Reading: Luke 1:1–4; John 20:30–31; 21:24–25
Poetry and Wisdom: Ps. 40:1–8
Second Reading: Acts 2:42; 2 Peter 1:12–14, 20–21; 3:1–2,
                      14–18

"So then you are no longer strangers and aliens, but you are citizens with the saints and also members of the household of God, built upon the foundation of the apostles and prophets, with Christ Jesus himself as the cornerstone." (Eph. 2:19–20)

———————————

Jesus read, quoted, and endorsed the Hebrew scriptures as the word of God. Jesus said, "Do not think that I have come to abolish the law or the prophets; I have come not to abolish but to fulfill. For truly I tell you, until heaven and earth pass away, not one letter, not one stroke of a letter, will pass from the law until all is accomplished" (Matt. 5:17–18; cf. Luke 16:16–17). There is a harmonious unity and agreement between the word of God in the OT and the words and teaching of Jesus. The written words of the OT provided the authority on which Jesus taught, challenged the religious leaders, and argued for the truth of God (e.g., Mark 12:24). Likewise, the apostles and early Christian teachers and preachers accepted the Old Testament as the word of God.

In the oldest Christian communities of the first century, there was immediately another authoritative word of God—the words and teachings of Jesus were told and retold in a living oral tradition. Of course the most trustworthy source for learning Jesus's teachings was the inner circle of Jesus's apostles or someone having a close relationship with one or more of the apostles (cf. Acts 2:42). However, the rapidly growing faith in Jesus Christ created a need for authoritative written documents whose authors would collect, arrange, narrate, and accurately preserve the stories of Jesus.

Luke states that he interviewed eyewitnesses who had personal, firsthand contact with Jesus. This included gathering sayings and stories retold by the apostles and others who had been close to Jesus. Though he was not personally an eyewitness, Luke gathered his information from primary sources, from those who had that privilege (cf. Luke 1:1–4).

There is broad agreement that the Gospel of Mark was the first of the four canonical gospels written, followed by Luke or Matthew and then John. Matthew and John were among the inner circle of the twelve apostles. However, Mark and Luke fit a secondary category. According to early church history, Mark, also known as John Mark (cf. Acts 12:12), was the traveling companion of Paul and Barnabas (Acts 12:25; 13:5; 15:37), and he later accompanied Peter the apostle. Papias, bishop of Hierapolis, wrote early in the second century (c. 130), "If ever any man came who had been a follower of the elders, I would enquire about the sayings of the elders; what Andrew said, or Peter, or Philip, or Thomas, or James, or John, or Matthew, or any other of the Lord's disciples." Concerning the Gospel of Mark, Papias reportedly added, "Mark became the interpreter of Peter and he wrote down accurately, but not in order, as much as he remembered of the sayings and doings of Christ" (Eusebius, *Ecclesiastical History*, 3.39.4 and 15). Other gospels were written, but over time the early church selected only four—the most accurate and faithful to the life and teaching of Jesus.

Paul, the apostle, was not one of the original Christian elders. However, during his lifetime, his leadership and wisdom became broadly recognized. For this reason, his letters were copied, circulated, and collected as a source of authoritative teaching among the young, growing churches (Col. 4:16). Very early, Peter acknowledged the value of Paul's letters to be on par with other holy writings: "Our beloved brother Paul wrote to you according to the wisdom given him ... There are some things in them hard to understand, which the ignorant and unstable twist to their own destruction, as they do the other scriptures" (2 Pet. 3:15f). There is evidence that supports a possible collection of Paul's thirteen letters plus the Letter to the Hebrews before the end of the first century.

The New Testament process of canonization of the twenty-seven books continued into the third century. Origen, a Christian teacher in Alexandria (c. 182–251), was the first to join the collection of the four gospels and the apostolic letters together with the title "New Testament." He mentions a continuing debate whether or not some books should be included or excluded from the canon. However, the list is very similar to the present twenty-seven books included in the Christian scriptures.

In summary, there appears to have been four standards used by the early church, especially by the leaders and councils, to select the twenty-seven books of the NT canon.

- ✓ *Content:* Consistent with the sayings of the Lord Jesus and the law and the prophets of the OT.
- ✓ *Apostolicity:* Written by an apostle or someone having a sustained relationship with an apostle so as to raise the book to apostolic status.
- ✓ *Catholicity:* Acknowledged broadly by a majority of the early churches as normative for Christian faith, life, and practice.
- ✓ *Inspiration:* The Holy Spirit inspired the author and reveals the truth of God to the listener/reader.

The New Testament canon includes the following twenty-seven books:

Gospels: Matthew, Mark, Luke, and John
History of the Church: The Acts of the Apostles

> *Pauline Letters or Epistles:* Romans, 1 and 2 Corinthians, Galatians, Ephesians, Philippians, Colossians, 1 and 2 Thessalonians, 1 and 2 Timothy, Titus, and Philemon
>
> *General Letters or Epistles:* Hebrews, James, 1 and 2 Peter, 1, 2, and 3 John, and Jude
>
> *Prophecy:* Revelation

Prayer:

Blessed Father of Jesus Christ, the living Word:

You continue to sustain, sanctify, and inspire your people with the gospels, history, letters, and vision of the scriptures.

For the New Testament is our beloved treasure of truth, preserving the cornerstone and foundation of our living faith. Amen.

Section 4

THE LORD'S PRAYER

Cf. Matthew 6:9–13 and Luke 11:2–4

Our Father in heaven,
    hallowed be your name.
Your kingdom come.
Your will be done,
    on earth as it is in heaven.
Give us this day our daily bread.
And forgive us our trespasses,
    as we forgive those who trespass against us.
And lead us not into temptation,
    but deliver us from evil.
For yours is the kingdom, and the power,
    and the glory forever and ever. *Amen.*

Week 4.3—Tuesday

Jesus Prayed

First Reading: Matt. 6:1, 5–8
Poetry and Wisdom: Ps. 86:1–11
Second Reading: Luke 18:1–14

"Jesus often withdrew to lonely places and prayed." (Luke 5:16 NIV)

———————

Jesus prayed. He withdrew to deserted places, where he could be alone with God the Father, without any distractions (Luke 5:16; 9:18; 22:41). He retreated to mountains (Mark 6:46; Luke 6:12; 9:28) and quiet gardens (Luke 22:39–41; John 18:1). He encouraged his followers to go to an inner room of the house—a room without windows—and shut the door (Matt. 6:6). Jesus prayed in quiet places free of earthly noises and distractions (Matt. 6:6). For this reason, Christians commonly pray with their eyes closed to shut out earthly distractions and enter the presence of their heavenly Father.

Jesus, however, commonly prayed with his eyes open, according to the gospels. When he took the five loaves and the two fish to feed the five thousand, "He looked up to heaven, and blessed and broke the loaves" (Mark 6:41). At the tomb of Lazarus, Jesus "looked upward" and prayed (John 11:41). Then he commanded Lazarus to come out of the tomb. When Jesus prayed for the disciples and those who would believe their message in his High Priestly Prayer (John 17:1–26), the gospel states, "He looked up to heaven" and prayed (17:1). Jesus's followers, on the other hand, commonly pray in the manner of the humble tax collector, who "would not even look up to heaven, but beat his breast, saying, 'God, be merciful to me, a sinner!'" (Luke 18:13).

Other than the High Priestly Prayer in John 17, the prayers of Jesus that are included in the gospels are quite brief (e.g., Mark 14:36, 39; John 11:41–42). However, the gospels also report that Jesus sometimes spent the night in prayer (Luke 6:12), and other references also suggest that Jesus prayed for more extended times (Luke 9:18, 29; 11:1). On the other hand, he warns his disciples "not to heap up empty phrases as the Gentiles do; for they think that they will be heard because of their many words" (Matt. 6:7). "Empty phrases" (NRSV) or "babbling" (NIV) describes a repetition of words or phrases, chanting magical formulas, or uttering meaningless sounds. Prayer is not mindless repetition of many words but a thoughtful and purposeful conversation with the heavenly Father. Prayer engages one's spirit and mind.

One may pray with audible words or in silence (e.g., 1 Sam. 1:13), in private or in public. The primary purpose of the Jerusalem temple was to serve as a sacred sanctuary—"a house of prayer for all nations" (Mark 11:17)—a holy place where everyone was welcome to enter and pray.

We pray in many and varied ways. It is not how long, how loud, or how many times in a day we pray, as if by some repetitious magic or manipulation to force the Almighty to hear and answer our petition. Why? "Your Father knows what you need before you ask him" (Matt. 6:8). The person who prays has the assurance that he or she is a child of the heavenly Father, and the Father will respond positively to his or her petitions.

Jesus Christ taught his followers how to pray by his example, his words, and his model prayer—The Lord's Prayer.

Prayer:
Our Father in heaven,
    hallowed be your name.
Your kingdom come.

Your will be done,
    on earth as it is in heaven.
Give us this day our daily bread.
And forgive us our trespasses,
    as we forgive those who trespass against us.
And lead us not into temptation,
    but deliver us from evil.
For yours is the kingdom, and the power,
    and the glory forever and ever. Amen.

Jesus Teaches Us How to Pray (Part I)

First Reading: Luke 11:1–13
Poetry and Wisdom: Ps. 8:1–9
Second Reading: Matt. 6:9–15

"Pray then in this way: Our Father in heaven, hallowed be your name. Your kingdom come. Your will be done, on earth as it is in heaven." (Matt. 6:9–10)

———————————————

Jesus taught his disciples how to pray by means of a model prayer, which is known as "The Lord's Prayer," or simply "Our Father." This brief prayer consists of two sections with three petitions in each. It teaches basic principles and a pattern of priorities for our petitions. In the early part of the second century, the church fathers instructed the Christian community to pray this simple and yet profound prayer "three times a day" (*Didache* 8:3). The prayer was associated with the followers of Jesus from the beginning, and it remains the common daily and community prayer of all Christians to this day.

God our Father has first place in the prayer. Our human petitions follow in the second section with "Give us this day …" The prayer addresses two profound questions: First, who is God and what is his creative purpose in the world? And the second, who are we and what is our purpose in the world? Both sections aspire for conformity to the will of God in the world and in the life of the one who prays.

"Pray then in this way!" (Matt. 6:9). It is an emphatic command and in the plural: "Therefore you [plural] are to pray …" From the

beginning, it is a community prayer. Even though the prayer may be recited in the secret and solitary privacy of one's own room, there is the reminder that the one who prays belongs to a Christian community—historic, contemporary, and embracing believers in all nations, tribes, peoples, and languages. The first person singular (i.e., "I" and "me") is inappropriate in this Christian family prayer. Observe the plural pronouns throughout the prayer: "our," "us," "we." We are members of a large believing family.

"Our Father in heaven": The invocation is *reverential*, for it is addressing the Almighty, the Creator of the universe. And yet it is also quite familial, creating a child-father imagery in a relationship of dependence, affirmation, and love. Those who follow Jesus and obey his commandments have become children of the heavenly Father (cf. Matt. 12:50). We pray with the confident assurance that we have a place in the heavenly family, and God will respond positively to our petitions. In fact, our heavenly Father knows what we need before we ask him (Matt. 6:8).

The kingdom of God: The first three petitions are parallel in form –

Your name be hallowed!
Your kingdom come!
Your will be done!

These three imperatives are emphatic in nature, and they are summarized in the concluding phrase: "As in heaven also on earth" (lit.). The petitions express a passionate longing for the heavenly sanctity and reign of God to become fully realized among the people on earth as it is in the heavenly realm. For this, all those who follow Jesus continually pray and pursue in word and deed until the end of the age.

The first petition grasps the understanding that there is no distinction between the name and the person. It recalls the third commandment, "You shall not make wrongful use of the name of the Lord your God" (Ex. 20:7). The name signifies the person. In this sense, the name of God, the kingdom of God, and the will of God have the same ethical implications for the disciples and the world. Wherever God is given his proper reverence and love, there is a submission to his authority and obedience to his commandments.

The first half of the prayer expresses a passionate and universal aspiration for God's kingdom to become a reality for all who populate the earth. It is a prayer for a transformed earth and people—the restoration of God's active reign over all his creation.

Prayer:
Holy Father of a great multitude, as innumerable as the stars of
    heaven, from every nation, from all tribes and peoples and
    languages:
We join with all your family of faith—beloved, redeemed, and
    adopted—lifting our voices in prayer with the saints, the living
    and dead,
Pleading for the salvation of all people,
    and the restoration of all creation to do your will. Amen.

Week 4.5—Thursday

Jesus Teaches Us How to Pray (Part II)

First Reading: Matt. 6:19–34
Poetry and Wisdom: Ps. 32:1–11
Second Reading: Matt. 18:21–35

"Pray then in this way ... Give us this day our daily bread. And forgive us our debts, as we also have forgiven our debtors. And do not bring us to the time of trial, but rescue us from the evil one." (Matt. 6:11–13)

———————————

Whereas the first half of the Lord's Prayer focused on the realm and reign of God or the kingdom of heaven, the three petitions in the second half focus upon the earthly existence and human quest of the believing community—the daily quest for food, forgiveness, and faithfulness.

The fourth petition, "Give us today our daily bread," recognizes the multiplied contingencies of life (e.g., sunshine, rain, drought, floods, health, sickness, employment, unemployment). Thus, the disciple prays to the heavenly Father for the food necessary for survival in the coming day. It is an affirmation of our continual dependence upon the grace and mercy of God. Bread may also imply all three basic needs—food, clothing, and shelter.

From one's relationship to the earth and survival, the fifth petition turns to the importance of harmonious relationships with God and others, "Forgive us our debts, as we also have forgiven our debtors." The gospels use three Greek words as interchangeable synonyms—debts (Matt. 6:12; 18:27), trespasses (Matt. 6:14; Mark 11:25), and sins (Matt. 18:21; Luke 11:4). A debt is an obligation that is owed. A trespass is a false step, a failure, a mistake, a blunder. A sin is a missing of the mark, a shortcoming, a failure to satisfy that which is expected of us by God and others.

The good news of the gospels is that God has taken the first step. In Jesus's sacrificial death on the cross, God has forgiven our debts and obligations to him. It is now our responsibility to likewise forgive the obligations of others owed to us (Matt. 6:14–15).

Jesus clarifies this point in the parable of the unforgiving debtor (Matt. 18:23–35). When a king wished to settle accounts with his official servants, he learned that one owed him ten thousand talents (ca. $7,000,000,000 USD).[1] The servant was unable to pay the account, so the king sentenced the servant to a lifetime of slavery, along with every member of his family. The man begged for patience and mercy, and in pity the king released the official and forgave his massive debt.

Subsequently, the forgiven official demanded that another man repay a debt of one hundred denarii owed to him (ca. $12,500 USD).[2] Unable to pay, the fellow servant, like the first, pled for patience and mercy. Denying the appeals, the official had his fellow debtor thrown into the paupers' prison until he could pay the debt. Learning of the official's despicable conduct, the king recalled the wicked servant to his court and reversed his prior judgment: "'You wicked slave! I forgave you all that debt because you pleaded with me. Should you not have had mercy on your fellow slave, as I had mercy on you?' And in anger his lord handed him over to be tortured until he would pay his entire debt" (Matt. 18:32–34). Jesus added, "So my heavenly Father will also do to every one of you, if you do not forgive your brother or sister from your heart" (Matt. 18:35).

"Forgive us our trespasses/debts" is a constant reminder and confession of our own sins and failures, and thus our perpetual need for divine forgiveness. Furthermore, as children of the heavenly

Father, we do as he does. As he forgives us, we also forgive those who have failed to fulfill their obligations to us.

The sixth petition concerning trials or temptations reminds every disciple of one's human nature and God-given desires, which must be constantly monitored, disciplined, and mastered. The petition appeals to the heavenly Father for divine protection and an escape from temptations and trials. However, should the test come, there is a passionate appeal for a divine deliverance from the evil or the evil one (i.e., Satan). It is a twofold petition—first, to avoid temptation, and second, to escape any evil consequences or moral stain.

Prayer:
Holy and loving Father:
You know what we need before we ask,
    and yet we are guilty of worries about life.
You have so graciously forgiven our trespasses and sins,
    and yet we are less forgiving toward the wrongs of others.
You have gifted us with passions and desires,
    and yet we squander them on worldly wealth and passing pleasures.
Have mercy, O Lord, and reign supremely in our lives this day.
    Amen.

[1] Talent = six thousand denarii/day's wages.
[2] Denarius = one day's wages (cf. Matt. 20:9).

Week 4.6—Friday

Christians Pray

First Reading: John 17:1–26
Poetry and Wisdom: Eccl. 5:1–6
Second Reading: Matt. 7:7–11

"For yours is the kingdom, and the power, and the glory forever and ever." (Matt. 6:13, annotation)

The concluding doxology of praise to God is not found in either gospel version of the Lord's Prayer (cf. Matt. 6:9–13; Luke 11:2–4). Rather, it is an ascription that appears as an addition in the later manuscripts of Matthew in the eighth and ninth centuries. A short form of the doxology is found in the late first or early second century text, *The Teaching of the Twelve Apostles*, aka *Didache*, "For thine is the power and the glory for ever" (8.2). These words echo the praise of King David in his prayer of farewell to Israel: "Yours, O Lord, are the greatness, the power, the glory ... [and] the kingdom" (1 Chron. 29:11).

When we pray, we are in the presence and in conversation with God Almighty. We speak *and* we listen. The Lord's Prayer teaches us to speak thoughtfully. We pray, not with many words and repetitious phrases (Matt. 6:7) but rather with purpose and understanding (cf. Eccl. 5:2; 1 Cor. 14:15). Prayer is more than getting things from God.

Where do we begin? With *adoration, praise, and thanksgiving!* We learn this through reading the Psalms, as well as in the recitation of the Lord's Prayer. For these are characteristic themes in the Psalms: "Bless the Lord ..." (Pss. 103 and 145), "Praise the Lord ..." (Pss. 113 and 150), and "Sing to the Lord ..." (Pss. 47 and 96). It is fitting that our prayers and worship commence with a holy recognition of our Creator, our heavenly Father—"O Lord, our Sovereign, how majestic is your name in all the earth!" (Ps. 8:1). That sounds like the first phrase of the Lord's Prayer, does it not?

When we come into the holy presence of our Lord, we experience an epiphany—a revelation of who we are—who we really are (Ps. 8:4). We are sinners in the presence of the Holy One (cf. Isa. 6:5; Luke 18:13). Therefore, we *confess our sins* and petition God for his divine mercy and forgiveness (1 John 1:9). Whenever there is true and honest confession and repentance of our sins, the Lord always responds with forgiveness and a refreshing baptism of his Spirit (Luke 18:14). Prayer cultivates and nurtures a life of humility, thanksgiving, and faith in Jesus Christ and the promises of God. We are the children of the heavenly Father.

As the children of God, we have confidence that he knows our needs before we voice our personal *petitions* (Matt. 6:8). Even though Jesus observed that a man was blind, he asked him, "What do you want me to do for you?" The blind man petitioned him, "My teacher, let me see again" (Mark 10:51). To the invalid lying near the pool of Beth-zatha, Jesus asked, "Do you want to be made well?" (John 5:6). Yes, our heavenly Father knows our needs; however, he desires that we ask him. Jesus tells us to state our requests in prayer: "Ask, and it will be given you; search, and you will find; knock, and the door will be opened for you. For everyone who asks receives, and everyone who searches finds, and for everyone who knocks, the door will be opened" (Matt. 7:7–8). There is power in prayer.

The high priestly prayer of Jesus in John 17 begins with Jesus's petitions for himself (17:1–5). His hour of suffering and death is imminent, and he prays that he might finish his mission to provide eternal life to all who believe. Subsequently, he *intercedes* for his disciples who will be left in the world to carry on their mission of representing Christ and proclaiming the gospel to the world (17:6–19). Then he prays for the church universal—all those who will believe the apostolic message in the days and years to come (17:20–26). He prays for the unity and effective witness of the church.

Adoration, thanksgiving, confession, petition, and intercession are five characteristic and common qualities observed in Christian prayers.

Prayer:
We magnify and praise the name of the Lord our God,
    who gives us breath, food for today, and a living hope.
Humbly we confess our failures to live and love,
    as Jesus has taught us by his life, teaching, and obedience.
Grant us the wisdom and courage to live by faith
    in life's valleys as well as on the successful summits.
Open the blinded eyes of those tapping and tripping through life
        to discover anew the redemptive love and purpose of our Creator. Amen.

Section 5

THE EARLY CREEDS
OF THE CHRISTIAN FAITH

The Shema
"Hear, O Israel: The Lord is our God, the Lord alone." (Deut. 6:4)

Judeo-Christian Belief in One God
"For us there is one God, the Father, from whom are all things and for whom we exist, and one Lord, Jesus Christ, through whom are all things and through whom we exist." (1 Cor. 8:6)

The Roman Confession
"If you confess with your lips that *Jesus is Lord* and believe in your heart that God raised him from the dead, you will be saved." (Romans 10:9)

The Corinthian Confession
"For I handed on to you as of first importance what I in turn had received: that *Christ died for our sins in accordance with the scriptures, and that he was buried, and that he was raised on the third day in accordance with the scriptures, and that he appeared to Cephas, then to the twelve.*" (1 Cor. 15:3–5)

THE ECUMENICAL CREEDS OF THE CHRISTIAN FAITH

The Apostles' Creed

I believe in God, the Father Almighty,

maker of heaven and earth;

I believe in Jesus Christ,
his only Son, our Lord:

who was conceived by the Holy Spirit,
born of the Virgin Mary,

suffered under Pontius Pilate,
was crucified, died, and was buried.

On the third day he rose again;

he ascended into heaven,
is seated at the right hand of the Father;
and will come again
to judge the living and the dead.

I believe in the Holy Spirit,

the holy catholic church,
the communion of saints,
the forgiveness of sins,

the resurrection of the body,
and the life everlasting. Amen.

The Nicene Creed

We believe in one God,
the Father, the Almighty,
maker of heaven and earth,
of all that is, seen and unseen.

We believe in one Lord, Jesus Christ,
the only Son of God,
eternally begotten of the Father,
God from God, Light from Light,
true God from true God,
begotten, not made,
of one Being with the Father;
through him all things were made.
For us and for our salvation
he came down from heaven,
was incarnate of the Holy Spirit and the
Virgin Mary,
and became truly human.
For our sake he was crucified under Pontius
Pilate;
he suffered death and was buried.
On the third day he rose again
in accordance with the Scriptures;
he ascended into heaven
and is seated at the right hand of the Father.
He will come again in glory
to judge the living and the dead,
and his kingdom will have no end.

We believe in the Holy Spirit,
the Lord, the giver of life,
who proceeds from the Father and the Son,
who with the Father and the Son
is worshipped and glorified,
who has spoken through the prophets.
We believe in one holy catholic and apostolic
church.
We acknowledge one baptism
for the forgiveness of sins.
We look for the resurrection of the dead,
and the life of the world to come. Amen.

Our Confession of Faith

First Reading: Deut. 6:4–9; 11:1, 18–21
Poetry and Wisdom: Ps. 119:57–72
Second Reading: 1 Cor. 15:1–11

"For I handed on to you as of first importance what I in turn had received: that Christ died for our sins in accordance with the scriptures, and that he was buried, and that he was raised on the third day in accordance with the scriptures, and that he appeared to Cephas, then to the twelve." (1 Cor. 15:3–5)

━━━━━━━━━━━━━

A creed is a declaration or confession of faith. This is what "I/we believe ..." (Latin, *credo*). It may be a brief statement of belief in only one God, such as the confession of Israel in the Shema, "Hear, O Israel: The Lord is our God, the Lord alone" (Deut. 6:4). Or a creed may assert a number of truths considered central and essential to an orthodox faith (e.g., the Apostles' and Nicene Creeds).

Following the example of Jesus, the ultimate authority for all Christian teaching and doctrine is the scriptures. Jesus corrected the error of the Sadducees, saying, "Is not this the reason you are wrong, that you know neither the scriptures nor the power of God?" (Mark 12:24). In fact, Jesus implies that the law and prophets—the Old Testament scriptures—are sufficient to convince the reader/ listener to believe in the power of God and repent from sin (Luke 16:29–31). From the first century, Christians have believed that "all scripture is inspired by God and is useful for teaching, for reproof, for correction, and for training in righteousness" (2 Tim. 3:16). However, all scripture is open for interpretation.

Therefore, one may anticipate a variety of interpretations. Each person comes to the study of the Bible with prior opinions, judgments, and beliefs. These presuppositions have been formed by our *culture* (e.g., ethnicity, political, social, economic, and religious background), *critical knowledge* (educational background in history, literature, language, natural abilities, life experiences, and age), and *character* (moral values, belief in the supernatural, human immortality, accountability, rational choices, and spiritual maturity). That is quite a list of personal abilities and/or disabilities, and the Bible warns us about the possibility of errors in one's own personal interpretations (2 Pet. 1:20). This brings us to the vital importance and role of the traditional ecumenical creeds, which define and declare some of the basic teachings of Jesus and the apostles.

In the gospels, Jesus asked his disciples, "Who do you say that I am?" Peter answered him, "You are the Messiah, the Son of the living God" (Matt. 16:16). Similarly, a creed is our response to the broad reading and study of God's word. It summarizes the major doctrines of the Bible, especially the teachings of the gospels.

After the death, resurrection, and ascension of Jesus, the Holy Spirit empowered the church to tell the world the good news of God. The Acts of the Apostles states that the early believers "devoted themselves to *the apostles' teaching* ..." (Acts 2:42). The gospels of Matthew and John are recognized as the truth and revelation of God from two of the twelve apostles. Mark and Luke received early acceptance as authoritative apostolic sources, because of Mark's relationship with the apostle Peter and Luke's investigation of eyewitness and apostolic accounts of the life and teaching of Jesus (cf. Luke 1:1–4).

The Apostles' Creed was not written by the apostles, nor can it be traced to an individual author. Rather, it is the development, growth, and collection of central truths historically founded upon the teachings of the apostles (Eph. 2:20). Its fragmented origins may be traced to second- and third-century oral forms, baptismal questions, and versions of "the faith." This early Latin creed provided the essential skeleton and framework for the elaboration and expansion by the First Ecumenical Council of Nicaea in AD 325.

The Nicene Creed originated out of theological controversies that threatened the very unity of the church in the fourth century. More than three hundred Christian bishops and hundreds of lesser clergy and laity assembled at Nicaea to clarify the nature of God and his divine revelation in Jesus Christ and the Holy Spirit. Therefore they affirmed and expanded the primitive Apostles' Creed with additional phrases for the purposes of clarification and correction of heresies. Later church councils have made some minor changes, but on the whole, the Nicene Creed remains unchanged after the Second Ecumenical Council convened in Constantinople in AD 381.

The Apostles' Creed: With other Christians of ages past and around the world, we now confess our living faith by means of the historic Apostles' Creed:

I believe in God, the Father Almighty,
> maker of heaven and earth.

I believe in Jesus Christ,
> his only Son, our Lord:
> who was conceived by the Holy Spirit,
> born of the Virgin Mary,
> suffered under Pontius Pilate,
> was crucified, died, and was buried.
> On the third day he rose again;
> he ascended into heaven,
> is seated at the right hand of the Father;
> and will come again
> to judge the living and the dead.

I believe in the Holy Spirit,
    the holy catholic church,
    the communion of saints,
    the forgiveness of sins,
    the resurrection of the body,
    and the life everlasting. Amen.

Week 5.1–Sunday

We Believe in One God

First Reading: Josh. 24:14–18
Poetry and Wisdom: Ps. 14:1–6
Second Reading: Acts 17:22–31

"For us there is one God, the Father, from whom are all things and for whom we exist, and one Lord, Jesus Christ, through whom are all things and through whom we exist." (1 Cor. 8:6)

Apostles' Creed: I believe in God ...
Nicene Creed: We believe in one God ...

———————————

"I believe in God" (Latin: *Credo in Deum*). This is a personal affirmation of faith. It is true *for me*. It is not the scientific language of description and analysis, or philosophical arguments and proofs that God exists. In fact, the Bible does not argue for the existence of God. Rather, the Torah begins simply, "In the beginning when God created the heavens and the earth ..." (Gen. 1:1). The Bible is a book of faith, and the creed begins and builds on this firm foundation. God is! God exists! Everything else that I believe depends upon the truth of this statement.

Whereas the Latin Apostles' Creed proclaims a personal commitment of faith, "*I* believe," the Greek Nicene Creed is communal, "*We* believe in one God" (Greek: πιστεύομεν εἰς ἕνα θεόν). As the believing community prays, "*Our* Father in heaven," we also confess with the words of the Nicene Creed: "*We* believe in one

84

God …" You and I belong to a community, a family of faith, the church. We stand with others who believe, trust, and strive to live in obedience to the will and purpose of God.

Christians are monotheists. When Jesus worshiped in his hometown synagogue in Nazareth or in the temple in Jerusalem, those assembled would likely have recited together their ancient creed: "Hear, O Israel: The Lord is our God, the Lord alone. You shall love the Lord your God with all your heart, and with all your soul, and with all your might" (Deut. 6:4f). Whereas other people and nations around them may have believed and worshiped other gods, the Jews worshiped the Lord their God alone who had brought their forefathers out of the land of Egypt and the house of slavery (Exod. 20:2). They chose to serve the Lord God who had made a covenant with their ancestors Abraham, Isaac, and Jacob (cf. Exod. 3:15; Deut. 29:13; Josh. 24:16).

We believe in one God. This is affirmed throughout the New Testament. "For us there is one God, the Father, from whom are all things and for whom we exist" (1 Cor. 8:6). "Is God the God of Jews only? Is he not the God of Gentiles also? Yes, of Gentiles also, since God is one; and he will justify the circumcised on the ground of faith and the uncircumcised through that same faith" (Rom. 3:29–30). "You believe that God is one; you do well. Even the demons believe—and shudder" (James 2:19; cf. Gal. 3:20; 1 Tim. 2:5).

Is this visible world all there is? We observe order, design, detail, grandeur, and purpose all around us in creation and nature. Yes, there is more! There is someone—a creator. We join with the psalmist, "The heavens are telling the glory of God; and the firmament proclaims his handiwork" (Ps. 19:1). The evidence for God—his power, his nature, his design—is so deliberately plain for all to see that it leaves no one with an excuse (Rom. 1:20). Yes, we believe in God who is revealed in creation, in scripture, and in his son, Jesus Christ.

When Paul the apostle was invited to address the leaders of Athens in the Areopagus, he acknowledged that they were a religious people. Like a tourist, he had observed their many altars and temples dedicated to their many gods. However, there was one altar dedicated "to an unknown god" (Acts 17:23). He proclaimed his faith in this one God, "The God who made the world and everything in it, he who is Lord of heaven and earth, does not live in shrines made by human hands, nor is he served by human hands, as though he needed anything, since he himself gives to all mortals life and breath and all things" (Acts 17:24f). The Athenians, like all people, were on a quest, searching to know this one, holy God who is over all gods (Acts 17:27). In their human ignorance, they overlooked the evidence all around them, and they did not believe or come to repentance.

This God, who revealed himself to Israel in the exodus, revealed himself to the Athenians and to all people in creation and in Jesus Christ who was raised from the dead.

Prayer:
You alone, O Lord, are God of gods and Lord of lords,
>the great God, mighty and awesome, creator of all that is;
>the God of truth and love, justice and mercy;
>the redeemer of all who believe, both Jew and Gentile.
You alone are worthy, our Lord and God,
>to receive glory and honor and our worship. Amen.

God, the Father

First Reading: Gen. 1:1–5; Exod. 3:13–15
Poetry and Wisdom: Ps. 68:1–6
Second Reading: Matt. 5:43–48; 7:21–23

"See what love the Father has given us, that we should be called children of God; and that is what we are." (1 John 3:1)

Apostles' Creed: I believe in God, the Father ...
Nicene Creed: We believe in one God, the Father ...

In the Old Testament, God is generally known by two names—God [*Elohim*, אֱלֹהִים] and Lord [*Yahweh*, אֶהְיֶה]. The first Hebrew name is plural, not a numerical or polytheistic plural of many gods but rather a plural of excellence, majesty, and complexity. Elohim sums up the many characteristics, attributes, and manifestations by which God is known to humanity. He is God Almighty, the God of creation.

Yahweh, on the other hand, was defined for Moses at the burning bush: "I am who I am" (Exod. 3:14). Moses was to say to the Israelites in Egypt that "I Am" had sent him as their deliverer. Yahweh is derived from the Hebrew verb "to be," "to exist." The Lord is "the one who is." The name implies that he is eternal, unchanging, always the same (i.e., "I was, I am, and I will be."). Yahweh is the Lord of the covenant with Israel.

God is also known as "father" in the Old Testament. In the song of Moses, God is the father of Israel: "I will proclaim the name of the Lord; ascribe greatness to our God! The Rock, his work is perfect, and all his ways are just. A faithful God, without deceit, just and upright is he ... *Is not he your father*, who created you, who made you and established you?" (Deut. 32:3–6). King David confessed, "You are my Father, my God, and the Rock of my salvation" (Ps. 89:26; cf. 103:13). The psalmist proclaims that God is the "father of orphans and protector of widows" (Ps. 68:5).

The prophets likewise referred to the Lord God as the loving father of Israel and all humanity: "You, O Lord, are our father; our Redeemer from of old is your name" (Isa. 63:16; cf. 64:8; Jer. 3:19; 31:9; Hos. 11:1–4; Mal. 1:6; 2:10). Isaiah proclaims that God the Father is the creator of all humanity, "O Lord, you are our Father; we are the clay, and you are our potter; we are all the work of your hand" (Isa. 64:8).

Christians believe that the God of the Old Testament is the one and same God of the New Testament. He is the Lord God to whom we pray, as Jesus taught us to say, "Our Father in heaven ..." Although references to the Father are not a common or major theme in the Old Testament, it becomes the primary name by which Jesus, the Son of God, explains his relationship to the Holy One who sent him. Especially in the Gospel of John, Jesus refers to God as "Father," "the Father" or "my Father" 127 times. The frequency is far less in the Synoptic Gospels (Matt., 43t; Mark, 4t; Luke, 15t), in which Jesus refers to the immortal, invisible, living God as "my/your Father," "my/your Father in heaven," and "my/your heavenly Father."

Historically, the father has been the typical head of the family. The title implies power, authority, and loving responsibility for the life and care of the family. For many, however, this parental character has been provided by their mother, perhaps due to an absentee or abusive father. Furthermore, in reality, God is spirit. God is neither male nor female.

Therefore, when "father" is used to support ecclesiastical sexism and a male-dominated power structure in the church or in civil politics, it must be challenged. In the church of Christ Jesus, there ought not to be ethnic, economic, or sexist superiority or inferiority. In Christ there is equality—"There is no longer Jew or Greek, there is no longer slave or free, there is no longer male and female; for all of you are one in Christ Jesus" (Gal. 3:28).

Prayer:
As your Son, our Savior, Jesus Christ, prayed,
    we also pray: "Abba! Father!"
For in love and mercy, you have redeemed us
    from our former slavery in sin and fear;
You have adopted us—all who believe—into your family.
    We are your children, the children of God the Father. Amen.

God, the Almighty

First Reading: Gen. 17:1–8
Poetry and Wisdom: Ps. 91:1–16
Second Reading: Rev. 19:1–16

"'I am the Alpha and the Omega,' says the Lord God, who is and who was and who is to come, the Almighty." (Rev. 1:8)

Apostles' Creed: I believe in God, the Father Almighty, maker of heaven and earth.

Nicene Creed: We believe in one God, the Father, the Almighty, maker of heaven and earth, of all that is, seen and unseen.

God appeared to Abraham, Isaac, and Jacob, saying, "I am God Almighty" (Gen. 17:1; 35:11; Exod. 6:3). This Hebrew name, *El–Shaddai*, means "God most powerful," "God omnipotent," or one who has universal, unlimited, infinite power and authority. He is the Lord God Most High "maker of heaven and earth" (Gen. 14:19, 22). In the Revelation to John, there is a repeated vision of the heavenly beings, the twenty-four elders, and the great multitude of the redeemed singing a song of adoration and worship: "Holy, holy, holy, the Lord God the Almighty, who was and is and is to come" (Rev. 4:8; cf. 11:17; 15:3; 16:7; 19:6).

From Genesis to Revelation, there is a resounding theme and proclamation: "We believe in one God, the Father, the Almighty." When the angel Gabriel made his announcement of God's favor to

Mary, she was perplexed and afraid. "How can this be, since I am a virgin?" (Luke 1:34). The angel responded, "The Holy Spirit will come upon you, and the power of the Most High will overshadow you; therefore the child to be born will be holy; he will be called Son of God" (Luke 1:35). How can this be? Christians respond in faith, "Nothing is impossible with God, the Almighty" (cf. Luke 1:37; 18:27; Matt. 19:26; Mark 9:23; 10:27; Gen. 18:14; Jer. 32:27).

We are the people of God, the people of possibilities. We pray, saying, "I believe; help my unbelief!" (Mark 9:24). Our prayers connect us to the infinite power and possibilities of God. Jesus said, "If you do not doubt in your heart, but believe that what you say will come to pass, it will be done for you. So I tell you, whatever you ask for in prayer, believe that you have received it, and it will be yours" (Mark 11:23–24). However, we also pray in humility and in harmony with the will of God, as Jesus prayed in the garden of Gethsemane before his arrest and trial: "Abba, Father, for you all things are possible; remove this cup from me; yet, not what I want, but what you want" (Mark 14:36).

God's omnipotence creates a theological tension for us. If God is all-powerful, does this open the door to fatalism and nullify free will? Is everything determined by God, leaving human beings powerless to choose or change our circumstances? Is human free will and the power of choice an illusion? Are we merely puppets on God's string? Actors in a divine comedy or tragedy?

The scriptures frequently remind us of God's power and eternal purposes, which may alter and determine personal decisions and the destinies of nations. Start with the Noahic Flood and God's covenant with Abraham. The pre–exodus plagues of Egypt are a well–known example of the mighty hand of God overruling the political purposes of Pharaoh (Exod. 6:1; 7:14; 12:31f). Samuel's choice of a successor to King Saul was the eldest son of Jesse, Eliab, who was tall, dark, and handsome. Instead, God chose David, Jesse's youngest, a handsome shepherd lad with reddish hair and complexion. God guided the wise men to Bethlehem to behold and worship the newborn Messiah

(Matt. 2:1–12), and God prevented King Herod from executing the infant Jesus (Matt. 2:13–18).

Jesus's life, death, and resurrection, in accordance with the prophetic scriptures and the eternal, detailed plan of the living God, forcefully remind us that he is God Almighty. The transformation of Saul—the persecutor and murderer of many early followers of the Way—into the great apologist and apostle Paul illustrates the providence and persuasive power of the living God (Gal. 1:13–17).

On the other hand, God created humankind in his own image with the ability to make choices (Gen. 1:26f). Certainly, with limitations, we are little creators. We make choices, and our decisions have consequences. Although our first parents were permitted to freely eat of every tree in the Garden of Eden, the tree of the knowledge of good and evil was declared off-limits by God (Gen. 2:16f). Sadly, Eve and Adam made an ill-fated choice having dire consequences for all generations that followed. Their disobedience and sin has affected the entire human family to this day.

From Genesis to Revelation, the scriptures continue a seamless narrative of God's revelation of his will and purpose and the human responsibility to choose—to ignore, to obey, or to disobey; to believe in God's son, Jesus Christ, or remain in our sin and unbelief. Our moral choices have consequences, or, as stated in the law, blessings or curses, joy or sorrow (cf. Deut. 28). It is only because we have free will that we can be held accountable by God for the outcomes in this present life and for eternity.

God Almighty and human free will are interwoven truths understood in tension. If a person over emphasizes the omnipotence of God at the expense of human free will, then God may become the author and source of sin, suffering, sorrow, hunger, inequality, war, and evil in the world. If one exults the freedom factor, then God's active presence and power in our world may be ignored and disregarded. We pray, for we truly believe that God Almighty is our source of wisdom, redemption, help, and hope.

Prayer (Rom. 11: 33–34 adapted):
O the mystery of the wisdom
    and knowledge of God Almighty!
How unsearchable are your judgments,
    and how inscrutable your ways!
For who has known the mind of the Lord,
    and who has been counselor to the Almighty?
Thus, we humbly bow in worship with a resolute will
    to continue your unfinished work in this imperfect world. Amen.

God, the Maker of Heaven and Earth

First Reading: Gen. 1:1–31
Poetry and Wisdom: Ps. 95:1–7
Second Reading: Rom. 1:16–25

"In the beginning when God created the heavens and the earth ..."
(Gen. 1:1)

Apostles' Creed: I believe in God, the Father Almighty, maker of
    heaven and earth.
Nicene Creed: We believe in one God, the Father, the Almighty,
    maker of heaven and earth, of all that is, seen and unseen.

———————————

God is spirit! Invisible? Yes. And yet his presence and activity is plain
for all to see. This is the declaration of Psalm 19:1–4,

> The heavens are telling the glory of God;
>   and the firmament proclaims his handiwork.
> Day to day pours forth speech,
>   and night to night declares knowledge.
> There is no speech, nor are there words;
>   their voice is not heard;
> yet their voice goes out through all the earth,
>   and their words to the end of the world.

All that is seen and unseen in the world around us reveals the nature and character of God. In modern terminology, nature is God's Word 1.0. Creation is "read-only," and the language is universal so that every living person can read it, sufficiently understand it, and thus know the living God. God's Word 2.0 is "read-write" in the covenant interaction with Israel in the Old Testament. God's Word 3.0 is "read-write-execute" in Christ, the grand revelation of God in human form for the salvation of all who believe. There is a divine-human connection in the cross and resurrection like no other.

The apostle Paul declares that Word 1.0 is sufficient for every living person to know God. He states, "For what can be known about God is plain to [all], because God has shown it to them. Ever since the creation of the world his eternal power and divine nature, invisible though they are, have been understood and seen through the things he has made. So they are without excuse" (Rom. 1:19–20).

The Nicene Creed adds the phrase "maker ... of all that is, seen and unseen." This is to refute the dualists who deem the body and the material creation as evil and exalt the human spirit as good. The creed is affirming that both have been created by God and were declared "very good." The exaltation of the unseen spirit over the physical body has promoted asceticism, celibacy, and the suppression of physical desires. Whereas in earlier times, this asserted the supremacy of the soul, modern science for many has replaced the immortal soul with the mind. According to modernity, the unseen world of faith, the soul, God, unclean spirits, miracles, and so forth are considered as nothing more than the superstitions of the gullible and less informed.

Too often people experience a "brain freeze" and attempt to arrive at a specific time—when? And how? When did God create the heaven and earth, all that is, seen and unseen? Was it 6,000 years ago, or six billion years ago? Is "day" in Genesis 1 a twenty-four-hour division of time, or does it denote a longer, perhaps much longer, span of time? It is certainly a general reference to a period or span of time in Genesis 2:4—"These are the generations of the heavens and the earth when they were created. In *the day* that the Lord God made the earth and the heavens."

Christians are optimistic realists. We acknowledge the presence of ancient marine fossils, embedded in hard rock formations deep in the earth and in the highest mountains far removed from oceans. The visible rock strata thrust upward in the mountains and lie openly exposed by erosion of wind and water to the naked eye in the Grand Canyon. Construction sites and archeological excavations continually uncover prehistoric skeletal remains of dinosaurs. Theories of evolution and survival of the fittest create more questions than answers, and yet the research and scientific quest fascinates our inquiring minds to know when and how heaven and earth came to exist.

The creeds circumvent the controversies that can divide: "We believe in one God, the Father, the Almighty, maker of heaven and earth, of all that is, seen and unseen." They do not answer our many human questions; rather, in faith the creeds declare, God did it! God is the creator of all that is. With this, Christians are in unanimous agreement.

Prayer:
How wonderful and marvelous are your works, O Lord.
You created heaven and earth, all that is, seen and unseen.
We are awed by the design, order, beauty and grandeur of it all.
Yet, marred by sin, suffering, and sorrow, all creation groans,
As do all your children, praying, eagerly longing, and anticipating
Your promised redemption, restoration, and return to reign supreme.
Amen.

One Lord, Jesus Christ

First Reading: Acts 4:1–12
Poetry and Wisdom: Ps. 118:19–29
Second Reading: Mark 8:22–33

"For us there is ... one Lord, Jesus Christ." (1 Cor. 8:6)

Apostles' Creed: I believe in Jesus Christ, his only Son, our Lord.
Nicene Creed: We believe in one Lord, Jesus Christ, the only Son
    of God.

———————————

With this meditation we enter the heart and central core of the two
ecumenical creeds. The longest of the three major sections affirms
the deity and humanity of Jesus Christ. In fact, the middle section
may be subdivided into two parts: the Son of God and the Son of
Man. The latter division begins with "for us and for our salvation
he came down from heaven ..." However, from the outset, the two
subdivisions are not to be separated, which makes this and the
following two meditations especially challenging.

    I. We believe in one God, the Father
   II. We believe in one Lord, Jesus Christ
      A. The Son of God (Divinity)
      B. The Son of Man (Humanity)
  III. We believe in the Holy Spirit

It should be noted that "one Lord" is parallel with "one God" in the opening line of the Nicene Creed. When the Old Testament was translated from Hebrew into the Greek Septuagint (LXX, third century BC), the Old Testament name for God, Yahweh, was translated *Kyrios* or Lord (cf. Gen. 2:8). Therefore, the Nicene Creed reminds us once again that Christians are monotheists, as the preface to today's text states, "There is no God but one" (1 Cor. 8:4). We believe in one Lord/one God who has revealed himself supremely in Jesus Christ.

The revelation or manifestation of God in Jesus Christ challenges our human comprehension, as it did the disciples of Jesus. In Mark's Gospel, Peter and his companions had witnessed at least fifteen miracles prior to Jesus's personal question, "Who do you say that I am?" (Mark 8:29). However, they failed to fully grasp the divinity of Jesus until after the resurrection.

The miraculous healing of the blind man of Bethsaida (Mark 8:22–26) is more than a miracle story, as it sets the stage for Jesus's question and Peter's failure to understand. It is a two-step miracle. Jesus put saliva on the blind man's eyes and laid his hands on him. When asked, "Can you see anything?" the man responded, "I can see people, but they look like trees, walking" (8:24). "Then Jesus laid his hands on his eyes again ... and his sight was fully restored, and he saw everything clearly" (8:25). Peter confessed in response to Jesus's question, "You are the Messiah" (8:29), but he failed to understand the purpose of Jesus, the Son of Man, who must experience rejection, crucifixion, and after three days rise again (8:31). Peter saw Jesus the man, but there was much more to see. His understanding of Jesus the Messiah, the Son of God, was unclear and baffling.

The suffering of Jesus can only be understood when a person sees beyond the physical humanity of Jesus and understands he is also truly divine, the Son of God. It was a process of discovery for the disciples that eluded their comprehension until after the resurrection. Even then, after encountering the risen Christ, some remained skeptical and doubted (cf. Matt. 28:17; Luke 24:22–27; John 20:25).

For many in our day, the incarnation of God in Jesus Christ becomes the stone that causes them to stumble (cf. Ps. 118:22; Matt. 21:42–44; Luke 20:17f; Acts 4:11f; Rom 9:32f; 1 Pet. 2:4–8). Jesus is the most popular teacher ever in human history, but he is more, much more, for he is the divine Son of God, our Lord.

Prayer:
Dear Lord and risen Savior:
Like Peter and friends,
    we too are on a pilgrimage of discovery.
The miracle stories of Jesus are familiar to us,
    And yet, like the skeptics present ages ago,
    we request one more sign, one more proof.
Please heal our blurry vision and wavering faith
    with another touch, another visit to the cross and empty tomb,
    that we might truly know Jesus Christ, the only Son of God. Amen.

Jesus Christ, the Son of God

First Reading: Col. 1:15–20
Poetry and Wisdom: Ps. 46:1–11
Second Reading: John 1:1–18

"No one has ever seen God. It is God the only Son, who is close to the Father's heart, who has made him known." (John 1:18)

Apostles' Creed: I believe in Jesus Christ, his only Son, our Lord.
Nicene Creed: We believe in one Lord, Jesus Christ, the only Son of God, eternally begotten of the Father, God from God, Light from Light, true God from true God, begotten, not made, of one Being with the Father; through him all things were made.

——————————

The nature of Jesus Christ—Son of God and Son of Man—has incited discussion, debate, and division within and outside the church from the first century to the present time. The internal clarification becomes quite evident in the fourth-century Nicene Creed with the addition of several corrective metaphors supporting the divine nature of Jesus Christ.

Mark's gospel begins and ends with the same assertion: "The beginning of the good news of Jesus Christ, the Son of God" (Mark 1:1), and it ends with the confession of the centurion at the cross observing the death of Jesus, "Truly this man was God's Son!" (Mark 15:39). Unclean demonic spirits recognized Jesus as the promised Messiah: "What have you to do with us, Jesus of Nazareth? Have you come to destroy us? I know who you are, the Holy One of God" (Mark 1:24; cf. 3:11; 5:7). Twice in Jesus earthly life, God the Father proclaimed the divine nature of Jesus Christ. At his baptism by John, God declared, "You are my Son, the Beloved; with you I am well pleased" (Mark 1:11; cf. Matt. 3:17; Luke 3:22). Again at the transfiguration, God said, "This is my Son, the Beloved; listen to him!" (Mark 9:7; Matt. 17:5; Luke 9:35).

Christology and the nature of Jesus Christ is a major theme in the Johannine writings. John's preface in the gospel asserts the eternal nature of Jesus, the Word: "In the beginning was the Word, and the Word was with God, and the Word was God" (John 1:1). Seven times in the creation story, God spoke the word, and order and life came to be (cf. Gen. 1). Jesus, the Word, the Son of God, is God, and John adds, "All things came into being through him, and without him not one thing came into being" (John 1:3). God the Father and God the Son are one and the same in nature. Jesus asserted, "Whoever has seen me has seen the Father" (John 14:9), and in another setting, he added, "The Father and I are one" (John 10:30; cf. 17:21, 22). In his high priestly prayer before his passion, Jesus reaffirmed his eternal and preexistent nature, "So now, Father, glorify me in your own presence with the glory that I had in your presence before the world existed" (John 17:5).

The divine nature and very essence of Jesus, the Messiah, is one and the same with the heavenly Father. There is not a time when he was not. We dare not think of his incarnation and infant birth to the Virgin Mary as his beginning, nor his passion as his end. He is the eternal, only begotten Son of God. Not a second deity but the manifestation and revelation of God himself in human flesh.

This is the very heart and kernel of the gospel. The reformer Martin Luther called John 3:16 the heart of the Bible, the gospel in miniature. Many Christians still quote the verse from the King James Version: "For God so loved the world, that he gave his only begotten Son, that whosoever believeth in him should not perish, but have everlasting life." What does "only begotten" mean? The

Greek word appears nine times in the New Testament (Luke 7:12; 8:42; 9:38; John 1:14, 18; 3:16, 18; Heb. 11:17; 1 John 4:9) and is a compound consisting of two words—*monos* = only, alone, unique; and *genos* = descendent, related, family. Jesus is the one and only one so uniquely born, having the very nature of God.

Therefore, in the Nicene Creed, we confess, "We believe in one Lord, Jesus Christ, the only Son of God, eternally begotten of the Father, God from God, Light from Light, true God from true God, begotten, not made, of one Being with the Father; through him all things were made." Jesus is Lord!

Prayer:
Lord Jesus Christ, the only Son of God:
You are the keystone in the arch,
    the cornerstone of the foundation,
      in the eternal plan of salvation for all who believe.
You came to bring life and light
    to our world of death and darkness,
      to show us the grace and redeeming love of God. Amen.

Jesus Christ, Our Savior

First Reading: Phil. 2:1–11
Poetry and Wisdom: Ps. 49:1–9
Second Reading: John 6:25–51

"I am the living bread that came down from heaven. Whoever eats of this bread will live forever; and the bread that I will give for the life of the world is my flesh." (John 6:51)

Apostles' Creed: No Parallel
Nicene Creed: For us and for our salvation he came down from heaven.

Why did God do it? For us! For you and me! For our salvation! Joseph was told to name Mary's son, "Jesus, for he will save his people from their sins" (Matt. 1:21; cf. Luke 1:31). As the ancient prophet Isaiah foretold, "'Look, the virgin shall conceive and bear a son, and they shall name him Emmanuel,' which means, 'God is with us'" (Matt. 1:23; cf. Isa. 7:14). When John the Baptist saw Jesus coming toward him, he declared to his disciples, "Here is the Lamb of God who takes away the sin of the world" (John 1:29). Yes, Jesus was more than a great teacher or another prophet sent by God. He was the Christ who came to save all humanity from their sins!

Jesus Christ is "God with us." "For us and for our salvation he came down from heaven." What does this mean? How a person answers the question may radically affect one's Christology and the meaning of salvation (i.e., soteriology).

Within the first century after the death and resurrection of Jesus, the Gnostics challenged the teachings of the apostles and the church fathers concerning the nature of Jesus Christ. The name comes from the Greek word *gnōsis*, meaning "to know, to have knowledge or wisdom." This philosophical quest for knowledge has its beginnings in the time of Plato (fourth century BC). The problem arose from a fundamental dualism that supposed the spirit to be good and the flesh to be evil. The Gnostics were troubled by the misery, suffering, and futility of human life in this physical world ruled by sin. The flesh with its evil desires must be suppressed. Many chose to escape the physical temptations—especially sex and material wealth— by fleeing to the barren desert regions to live out their lives in a lonely, monastic existence. For such men, marriage, procreation, and engagement in business for material wealth were evil. Celibacy, even castration, was exulted.

Gnostic dualism creates major problems concerning the nature of Jesus Christ. In their view, a holy God cannot be united, commingled, or become incarnate with corrupt, sinful human flesh. This leads to several possible explanations and theological errors.

First, the Savior only appeared to have a physical, human body. This heresy is called Docetism (*dokeō*), meaning "to seem." John's Gospel and Epistles certainly challenge this early error. Remember the proof Jesus provided Thomas after the resurrection, since he was not present to witness the first appearance of Jesus to his disciples. Thomas said, "Unless I see the mark of the nails in his hands, and put my finger in the mark of the nails and my hand in his side, I will not believe" (John 20:25). Therefore, when Jesus appeared to his disciples the second time a week later, he said to Thomas, "Put your finger here and see my hands. Reach out your hand and put it in my side. Do not doubt but believe." With this physical proof, Thomas confessed, "My Lord and my God!" (John 20:27–28). The evangelist Luke states that the risen Lord invited all those present for his first appearance to touch him, and he ate a piece of broiled fish to prove that he was not a ghost (Luke 24:36–43).

In his First Epistle, John calls the Docetists, antichrists, for they deny the human nature and physical body of the Savior:

> Beloved, do not believe every spirit, but test the spirits to see whether they are from God; for many false prophets have gone out into the world. By this you know the Spirit of God: every spirit that confesses that Jesus Christ has come in the flesh is from God, and every spirit that does not confess Jesus is not from God. And this is the spirit of the antichrist, of which you have heard that it is coming; and now it is already in the world. (1 Jn. 4:1–3; cf. 1:1–3; 2:18)

The incarnation of the Son of God continues to be a perplexing challenge for the human mind to grasp from the first century to the present. In the gospel reading for today, Jesus's listeners were puzzled, saying, "Is not this Jesus, the son of Joseph, whose father and mother we know? How can he now say, 'I have come down from heaven'?" (John 6:42). Jesus had multiplied seven loaves of bread and two fish, making the food sufficient to satisfy the hunger of a large crowd numbering as many as five thousand men, plus women and children (John 6:1–14; Mark 6:30–44). They had witnessed a very physical Jesus multiply physical bread that they could eat.

This provided Jesus with a teachable moment. Jesus's multiplication of the loaves of bread and the manna eaten by their ancestors during the exodus were gifts of God. The bread served as a sign, a metaphor, of something much greater for his listeners to understand. Jesus declared, "I am the bread of life ... the living bread that came down from heaven. Whoever eats of this bread will live forever; and the bread that I will give for the life of the world is my flesh" (John 6:35, 48, 51). Our Savior came down from heaven (cf. John 6:33, 38, 50, 51, 58), as the creed declares, and he became one of us, incarnate, in human flesh.

Prayer:
Blessed Lord, our Savior and Redeemer:
With purposeful humility you came into our world,
   taking the form of a servant,
   being born in human likeness, and
   becoming obedient to the point of death on the cross.
Therefore, we bow our knees in worship
   at the name that is above every name,
   confessing that Jesus Christ is Lord,
   To the glory of God the Father. Amen.

Jesus Christ, the Son of Man

First Reading: Isa. 7:14; 9:2–7; 11:1–3
Poetry and Wisdom: Job 9:1–3, 14–15, 19–20, 32–33
Second Reading: Luke 1:26–38; 11:27–28

"The angel said to [Mary], 'The Holy Spirit will come upon you, and the power of the Most High will overshadow you; therefore the child to be born will be holy; he will be called Son of God.'" (Luke 1:35)

Apostles' Creed: Who was conceived by the Holy Spirit, born of the Virgin Mary.

Nicene Creed: Was incarnate of the Holy Spirit and the Virgin Mary, and became truly human.

As in the previous meditation, the Nicene Creed supplements the Apostles' Creed with words that reaffirm the physical, human nature of Jesus Christ: "The Son of God ... who was true God from true God ... of one being with the Father ... [who] came down from heaven, was *incarnate* ... and *became truly human.*" This again alludes to the early heresies of the Gnostics and Docetists who taught that a holy God could not be joined or become incarnate in human flesh. Rather, they asserted that Jesus was a phantom, only appearing or seeming to be human. Their error or heresy develops from a dualism that supposed the spirit to be good and the flesh to be evil. At its root is either a rejection of the earlier creedal affirmation that God is the creator "of all that is, seen and unseen," or a failure to recognize the transforming presence of the Holy Spirit in the incarnation of Christ.

Ignatius, the bishop of Antioch (ca. AD 112) called the preachers of Docetism "wicked ... wild beasts ... [and] ravening dogs." He countered their error with the affirmation, "There is one Physician [i.e., healer], who is both flesh and spirit, born and yet not born, who is God in man, true life in death, both of Mary and of God, first passible [i.e., subject to suffering] and then impassible [i.e., incapable of suffering], Jesus Christ our Lord" (*To Eph.* 7.2). The apostle John called such teachers "antichrists"—that is, adversaries of Christ (1 John 2:18, 22). How are they known? By one basic test, "Every spirit that confesses that Jesus Christ has come in the flesh is from God, and every spirit that does not confess Jesus is not from God" (1 John 4:2f; cf. 2 John 1:7).

Luke's gospel affirms Mark's theological emphasis upon the divine nature of Jesus Christ—the miracle worker and Son of God—by incorporating as much as 53 percent of the earlier gospel. However, Luke augments Mark's account with extensive evidence for Jesus's human nature. Luke includes the story of Jesus's conception (1:26–38), birth (2:1–21), circumcision (2:21), dedication in the temple (2:22–40), precocious youthful engagement with the teachers in the temple (2:41–52), time in human history (3:1–2), and his human genealogy (3:23–38). Whereas Mark gives only two verses to Jesus's temptation experience, Luke expands the account to thirteen verses (4:1–13). Again, in contrast to Mark's account, Luke's first story following Jesus's temptation tells of his participation in the synagogue worship on the Sabbath in his hometown of Nazareth, which climaxes with mob rejection and an attempt on his life (4:16–30). What was their problem? How could Jesus, the son of Joseph and Mary, dare to claim that he was the Messiah foretold by the prophet Isaiah (4:21–22)? They knew Jesus as one of their village sons who had played in their streets and learned his father's trade as a craftsman. Jesus was truly human.

The temptation story (Luke 4:1–13) reminds us that Jesus was human and vulnerable to temptation. As the hour of his passion drew near, he was tempted to escape the suffering and imminent death on the cross. Thus he prayed, "Father, if you are willing, remove this cup from me; yet, not my will but yours be done." In his anguish, we are told that he prayed more earnestly, and his sweat became like great drops of blood falling down on the ground (Luke 22:42–44). The divine Son of God was truly human.

Jesus Christ was truly human but without sin. This is the miracle of the incarnation. In the annunciation to Mary, Gabriel declared, "The Holy Spirit will come upon you, and the power of the Most High will overshadow you; therefore the child to be born will be holy" (Luke 1:35). Certainly, Mary was highly favored and privileged to be chosen as the mother of the holy child (Luke 1:28, 30, 42). Of all the women who have ever lived, Mary has been the most highly favored by the "Lord God, Most High." She is worthy of honor, for she received the call of God and obeyed it (Luke 11:28).

At the home of her relative Elizabeth, Mary broke into a song of thanksgiving and praise to God, which is known as the Magnificat, saying, "My soul magnifies the Lord, and my spirit rejoices in God my Savior, for he has looked with favor on the lowliness of his servant ..." (Luke 1:46–48). Yes, Mary, like all humanity, longed for a savior who would save us from sin and death. Jesus Christ became our mediator, our Savior, for he alone could restore our broken relationship with a holy God.

Prayer: The Magnificat (Luke 1:46–55)
My soul magnifies the Lord
    and my spirit rejoices in God my Savior,
    for he has looked with favor on the lowliness of his servant.
Surely, from now on all generations will call me blessed;
    for the Mighty One has done great things for me,
    and holy is his name.
His mercy is for those who fear him

from generation to generation.
He has shown strength with his arm;
   he has scattered the proud in the thoughts of their hearts.
He has brought down the powerful from their thrones,
   and lifted up the lowly;
   he has filled the hungry with good things,
   and sent the rich away empty.
He has helped his servant Israel,
   in remembrance of his mercy,
   according to the promise he made to our ancestors,
   to Abraham and to his descendants forever. Amen.

The Passion of Christ

First Reading: Rom. 5:6–11
Poetry and Wisdom: Ps. 85:1–9
Second Reading: John 18:28–32; 19:1–42

"God proves his love for us in that while we still were sinners Christ died for us." (Rom. 5:8)

Apostles' Creed: Suffered under Pontius Pilate, was crucified, died and was buried.
Nicene Creed: For our sake he was crucified under Pontius Pilate; he suffered death and was buried.

———————————

Why did Jesus Christ voluntarily submit to his arrest, religious and civil trials, crucifixion, death, and burial? His passion or suffering was "for our sake" (Rom. 5:6–8). This phrase added in the Nicene Creed reinforces the prior phrase, "For us and for our salvation he came down from heaven." You and I, all humanity, were on God's mind and heart from the beginning (cf. 2 Cor. 5:21; 1 Pet. 1:20). Jesus suffered and died for you and for me. Why? Love made him do it (John 3:16; cf. Mark 10:45; Luke 19:10).

God's plan and passion for our redemption was foretold in the scriptures. On the day of Jesus's resurrection, he joined two very sad and perplexed disciples on the way to Emmaus. He listened attentively to their accounting of the events of the past three days and their dashed hopes (Luke 24:21). And yet that very day some of their comrades reported that the tomb was empty, and the body of Jesus was gone. With that, Jesus chided them for being so slow to believe. The answer was found in the scriptures: "Then beginning with Moses and all the prophets, [Jesus] interpreted to them the things about himself in all the scriptures" (Luke 24:27).

God's plan of salvation was predetermined, prophesied, and precise (cf. Mark 1:15; Gal. 4:4). The events transpired in verifiable history. Jesus was born during the latter reign of King Herod (Matt. 2:1; Luke 1:5; ca. 4 BC). He began his public ministry "In the fifteenth year of the reign of Emperor Tiberius, when Pontius Pilate was governor of Judea, and Herod [Antipas] was ruler of Galilee ... during the high priesthood of Annas and Caiaphas" (Luke 3:1–2; ca. AD 28). The majority of scholars conclude that Jesus died in either AD 30 or 33, when the Passover would have fallen on the Sabbath, making it "a day of great solemnity" (John 19:31). Like the lamb that was to be slain on the day of Preparation for the Passover (Mark 14:12), Jesus was crucified and died before sunset and the beginning of the Passover/Sabbath.

Rather than death by stoning (cf. Lev. 24:16, 23; Deut. 13:10; John 8:5; Acts 7:59), the Jewish leaders demanded that Pontius Pilate sentence Jesus to death by crucifixion. Why? The law stated, "When someone is convicted of a crime punishable by death and is executed, and you hang him on a tree [i.e., stake, pole, cross], his corpse must not remain all night upon the tree; you shall bury him that same day, for anyone hung on a tree is under God's curse" (Deut. 21:22f).

Death by crucifixion was a gruesome, slow, painful execution—the ultimate sign of public shame and scorn reserved for slaves, fugitives, foreign captives, and rebels. Appian, the Roman historian, reports that the Roman general Crassus captured six thousand survivors of Sparticus's slave rebellion in 71 BC. As a deterrent against future rebellions in the empire, he marched the POWs to Rome, where they were crucified on crosses lining the road from Rome to Capua (*Civil Wars*, 1.120). The Jewish leaders accused Jesus of blasphemy—asserting that he was the Messiah, Son of God—and thus worthy of the most excruciating form of public punishment (Mark 14:61–64; Luke 22:66–71; John 19:7).

By late afternoon on Good Friday, Jesus was dead. When the soldiers came to break the legs of those crucified in order to accelerate their deaths by asphyxiation, they concluded that Jesus was already dead. Therefore, they did not break his legs, as the scriptures foretold (John 19:36; cf. Exod. 12:46; Num. 9:12; Ps. 34:20). "Instead, one of the soldiers pierced his side with a spear, and at once blood and water came out" (John 19:33f). There were no spurts of bright arterial blood but rather semisolid clots and watery serum, according to an eyewitness (John 19:35). This indicated that Jesus had been dead for some time. The supervising centurion, having witnessed Jesus's suffering and death, confessed, "Truly this man was God's Son!" (Mark 15:39; Matt. 27:54).

The inclusion of the women disciples observing Jesus's crucifixion and death at a distance from the cross also served to authenticate Jesus's death (Mark 15:40f). On the first day of the week, the women came to the tomb with spices to anoint Jesus's body, for they concluded that Jesus had indeed died (Mark 16:1). To this growing list of witnesses, the compassionate burial duo of Joseph of Arimathea and Nicodemus, members of the Jerusalem Council, may also be added (John 19:38–42; cf. 3:1; 7:45–52).

Jesus was not in a temporary swoon or a coma. Jesus, the Son of God, was dead! His body was wrapped with a mixture of expensive burial spices (about one hundred pounds) in a linen shroud. His mummified body was then placed in the tomb in accordance with Jewish burial customs (John 19:39–40).

Prayer:
The passion of our Lord arrests our restless thoughts,
Calling us to pause in quiet meditation, often with tears,
    for Jesus Christ, the Lamb of God, suffered and died
    to take away the sin of the world.
Yes, this is God's grand story, his story of love,
    for all humanity; yes, for even me. Amen.

Week 6.3—Tuesday

The Resurrection of Christ

First Reading: 1 Cor. 15:1–11
Poetry and Wisdom: Ps. 42:1–11
Second Reading: John 20:1–22

"Christ died for our sins in accordance with the scriptures, and that he was buried, and that he was raised on the third day in accordance with the scriptures, and that he appeared to Cephas, then to the twelve. Then he appeared to more than five hundred brothers and sisters at one time." (*The Corinthian Confession*, 1 Cor.15:3–6)

Apostles' Creed: On the third day he rose again.
Nicene Creed: On the third day he rose again in accordance with the Scriptures.

———————

To prevent a possible scandal worse than the first, the Jewish leaders went to Pilate asking that the tomb be made secure for three days. They had heard Jesus say, "After three days I will rise again" (Matt. 27:63). The leaders feared any possible plot, rumor, or report suggesting that Jesus's body was gone and the tomb was empty. Pilate granted their request, and the entrance to the tomb, which had been carved out of the rock, was closed with a large rolling stone, sealed so as to disclose any tampering, and a twenty-four-hour guard of soldiers was assigned to keep watch.

On the morning following the Passover-Sabbath, all four gospels report that the stone had been rolled away from the entrance and the tomb was empty (Matt. 28:1, 5–7; Mark 15:1–7; Luke 24:1–8; John 20:1–10). Jesus's body was gone? Had his body been moved by his opponents? By the guards? By the disciples? The former could later produce the body to debunk the disciples' proclamation of Jesus's resurrection. Matthew reports that the priests conspired with the guards, giving them a large sum of money to spread the story that Jesus's disciples came by night and stole the body while we were asleep (28:11–15). However, sleeping on duty was a serious charge, possibly punishable by death. If someone had stolen the body, the corpse would have remained wrapped in the linen shroud for final burial. Instead, the burial clothes remained in the tomb, as if the body had evaporated (John 20:6f).

The presence of the women at the cross, observing the burial, and the first to discover the empty tomb supports the authenticity of the gospel account. Jesus chose the twelve disciples, who were all men. When Jesus twice fed the multitudes, Matthew states that there were about 5000 and 4000 men, "besides women and children" (14:21; 15:38). If someone were writing a fictional story of the resurrection, the first person to discover the empty tomb and see the risen Lord would have been preeminent Peter, or at the least one of the twelve disciples. Instead, the discovery of the empty tomb was made by the women—yes, women disciples—who had followed Jesus from Galilee.[1]

At the dawn of the first day of the week, Mary Magdalene, Mary the mother of James, and Salome went to the tomb, found the large stone rolled back, entered the tomb, and discovered that the body of Jesus was gone. An angel announced the amazing news, "I know that you are looking for Jesus who was crucified. He is not here; for he has been raised, as he said. Come, see the place where he lay. Then go quickly and tell his disciples, 'He has been raised from the dead'" (Matt. 28:5–7). The inclusion and important role of the women is unusual in the literature of the time. It is of further interest that Paul does not mention any appearances of the risen Christ to women followers. In the gospels, the women are models of faith and obedience (Matt. 28:8; Luke 24:9).

The four gospels, Acts, and Paul's letters include as many as eleven post-resurrection appearances of the risen Lord to his disciples.[2] In the seven weeks from Easter to Pentecost, the disheartened, doubting disciples were transformed and so convinced of the resurrection that they were willing to die for Jesus Christ. On the day of Pentecost, Peter boldly proclaimed, "Jesus of Nazareth, a man attested to you by God with deeds of power, wonders, and signs that God did through him among you, as you yourselves know—this man ... you crucified and killed ... but God raised him up" (Acts 2:22–24).

Faith in the resurrection of Jesus Christ is at the very heart and core of the Christian faith. As Paul states, "If Christ has not been raised, then our proclamation has been in vain and your faith has been in vain ... And you are still in your sins" (1 Cor. 15:14–17). Good Friday and Easter are the source of our peace with God and our confident hope for life eternal.

Prayer:
All praise to you, our risen and living Lord:
The stone was rolled away, your body was gone;
Only the linen burial shroud remained.
Sin's curse and the fear of death were conquered that day.
With the saints of ages past, we join the triumphal procession,
A victory parade celebrating life and hope beyond the grave. Amen.

---

[1] More than six women appear in the crucifixion and resurrection accounts: (1) Mary, Jesus's mother, (2) his mother's sister, (3) Mary, the wife of Clopas, (4) Mary Magdalene, (5) Mary, the mother of James the younger and Joseph, (6) Salome, possibly the wife of Zebedee and mother of James and John, and (7) many other women (cf. John 19:25; Matt. 27:55f, 61; 28:1; Mark 15:40f, 47; Luke 23:49, 55; 24:10).

[2] The eleven post-resurrection appearances of the risen Lord: Mary Magdalene (John 20:11–18; [Mark 16:9]); the women (Matt. 28:9–10); Simon Peter

(Luke 24:34; 1 Cor. 15:5); two disciples on Emmaus Road (Luke 24:13–32; [Mark 16:12–13]); ten disciples (Luke 24:36–49; John 20:19–23; 1 Cor. 15:5); eleven disciples (John 20:26–29; [Mark 16:14]); seven disciples (John 21:1–14); eleven disciples (Matt. 28:16–20); more than 500 (1 Cor. 15:6); James (1 Cor. 15:7); and the disciples at the ascension (Luke 24:50–52; Acts 1:3–11).

The Ascension of Christ

First Reading: John 17:1–5; Matt. 28:16–20
Poetry and Wisdom: Ps. 110:1
Second Reading: Luke 24:44–53; Acts 1:1–11

"The Lord says to my lord, 'Sit at my right hand until I make your enemies your footstool.'" (Ps. 110:1)[1]

Apostles' Creed: Jesus Christ ... ascended into heaven, is seated at the right hand of the Father.

Nicene Creed: Jesus Christ ... ascended into heaven and is seated at the right hand of the Father.

The physical presence of Jesus in our world of time and space is transformed in the miracle of the resurrection. Yes, he appears to the disciples and to as many as five hundred at one time after the resurrection, but in these manifestations he is different. When he appeared to the weeping Mary Magdalene in the garden, and she desired to grasp and hold him, Jesus said, "Do not hold on to me, because I have not yet ascended to the Father. But go to my brothers and say to them, 'I am ascending to my Father and your Father, to my God and your God'" (John 20:17).

When Jesus was recognized in the blessing and breaking of bread by the two disciples in Emmaus, Luke reports, "He vanished from their sight" (Luke 24:31). Later, that evening, he appeared and stood among the ten disciples, even though "the doors were locked for fear of the Jews" (Luke 24:36; John 20:19). Jesus was not a ghost and insisted that the disciples look and even touch the scars in his hands and feet (Luke 24:39; John 20:27). He also ate a piece of broiled fish in their presence (Luke 24:42f). Seeing and touching the risen Christ was the convincing proof for Thomas especially, who then believed that Jesus had indeed been raised (John 20:27).

Only Luke reports the ascension of Jesus Christ forty days after his resurrection: "After his suffering he presented himself alive to them by many convincing proofs, appearing to them during forty days and speaking about the kingdom of God" (Acts 1:3). Furthermore, Luke gives two accounts of the ascension (Luke 24:50f; Acts 1:9). The first brings the gospel to a close, while the second provides the commission for the disciples and the church empowered by the ever-living Christ.

Although the gospels of Matthew and Mark allude to the exaltation and reign of Jesus Christ with God the Father, they do not mention how he came to be in heaven (Matt. 16:27; 24:30; 26:64; Mark 8:38; 13:26). John likewise refers to Jesus as the one who descended or came down from heaven, and he ascended or returned to the father in heaven (John 3:13; 6:62; 13:1–13; 16:5; 16:28; 20:17). It is in John that Jesus uses the term "to be lifted up" (John 3:14; 8:28; 12:32–34). Commonly, Christians think of Jesus as being lifted up on the cross, which is certainly true. However, it may also include his ascension, exaltation, and glorification in the presence of God the Father, which was his before the beginning of time and creation (John 17:5; 12:16, 23).

Although the ascension is specifically reported as a visible event in time and space only in the Gospel of Luke and Acts, the exaltation and heavenly reign of Jesus Christ was essential in the earliest Christian theology. This is witnessed in the pre-Pauline "Christ Hymn" of the church, as quoted in Paul's Letter to the Philippians: "God also highly exalted him and gave him the name that is above every name, so that at the name of Jesus every knee should bend, in heaven and on earth and under the earth, and every tongue should confess that Jesus Christ is Lord, to the glory of God the Father" (2:9–11).

God is spirit! And God is one! The earthly, physical imagery used to describe the ascended, exalted, and enthroned Christ as "seated at the right hand of the Father" (e.g., Col. 3:1)[2] may be misconstrued by some to understand the theology of the Trinity as a belief in three gods. This is not so! We believe in one God, who has made, and continues to make, himself known to us in three forms— Father, Son, and Holy Spirit. Rather, the time and space imagery is used to indicate that Jesus Christ sits, stands, reigns in the place of highest honor, majesty, authority, and power in the redemptive plan of the living God. Christians now await our ascended Lord's return or Second Advent (Matt. 24:30f).

Prayer:
With the saints of the ages—
　a great multitude that no one can count,
　from every nation, from all tribes and peoples and languages—
We too bend our knee in worship of the exalted Lamb of God;
　and with our tongues we confess that Jesus Christ is Lord,
To the glory of God the Father. Amen.

---

[1] Psalm 110:1 is quoted more often in NT than any other OT verse (e.g., Matt. 22:44; Mark 12:36; Luke 20:42f; Acts 2:34f; 1 Cor. 15:25; Eph. 1:20; Heb. 1:3, 13; 10:12f).

[2] Acts 2:33–35; 5:31; 7:55f; Rom. 8:34; Eph. 1:20f; Col. 3:1; Heb. 1:3, 13; 8:1; 10:12; 12:2; 1 Pet. 3:22.

The Second Coming

First Reading: Rev. 1:1–8
Poetry and Wisdom: Ps. 53:1–6
Second Reading: Matt. 24:1–31, 36

"Then the sign of the Son of Man will appear in heaven, and then all the tribes of the earth will mourn, and they will see 'the Son of Man coming on the clouds of heaven' with power and great glory." (Matt. 24:30)

Apostles' Creed: Jesus Christ … will come again.
Nicene Creed: Jesus Christ … will come again in glory.

The period beginning four Sundays before Christmas is widely observed by Christians as the season of Advent. It is a season of joy and celebration of Christ's first advent and birth in Bethlehem. It is also a time to emphasize the promised return of the Savior— Christ's Second Coming, Advent, or Parousia. This latter emphasis calls believers to prayer and preparation for his return and the final judgment of the living and the dead.

The Second Coming will not be a secret appearing to an elect or chosen few. In the Revelation, John writes, "Look! He is coming with the clouds; every eye will see him, even those who pierced him; and on his account all the tribes of the earth will wail. So it is to be" (1:7). In the words of Jesus to the disciples, "The sign of the Son of Man will appear in heaven, and then all the tribes of the earth will mourn, and they will see 'the Son of Man coming on the clouds of heaven' with power and great glory" (Matt. 24:30).

It is true that the early church lived on tiptoe with anticipation that Christ's coming would occur very soon, possibly during the lifetimes of the first-century believers. Some mistakenly thought that he may have already come, and they missed it. Thus, some became quite troubled. Paul calmed the fear of the believers in Thessalonica: "As to the coming of our Lord Jesus Christ and our being gathered together to him, we beg you, brothers and sisters, not to be quickly shaken in mind or alarmed, either by spirit or by word or by letter, as though from us, to the effect that the day of the Lord is already here" (2 Thess. 2:1–2). This hyper-anticipation of the imminent return of the Savior caused some to live in idleness and presume upon the generosity of others for food (cf. 2 Thess. 3:6, 11–12).

The Synoptic Gospels (Matt. 24; Mark 13; Luke 21) preserve and proclaim Jesus's teaching concerning his Second Coming in what is sometimes called the Little or Gospel Apocalypse. Like the first disciples, we also want to know the time and means by which we will be able to discern our Lord's return (Matt. 24:3). Jesus answers with several warnings that no one be led astray by any signs. There will be many charismatic and prophetic charlatans who will come claiming to be Christ the Messiah, and they will lead many astray. There will be wars and rumors of wars, nation will rise against nation, famines and earthquakes will occur, Christians will be tortured and martyred, but the one who endures to the end will be saved (Matt. 24:13). It will be necessary for some to flee for their lives and live as aliens in exile to survive (Matt. 24:15–24).

Christians are warned not to lose hope during this interim time—short or long—between the First and Second Advent. During this time of hope and anticipation, the good news of the kingdom will be proclaimed throughout the world as a testimony to all the nations (Matt. 24:14).

Again the Christian is reassured that "as the lightning comes from the east and flashes as far as the west, so will be the coming of the Son of Man" (Matt. 24:27). Jesus Christ will appear with power and great glory, and all the tribes of the earth will mourn, for they have been forewarned and remain unprepared for his coming.

Jesus gives all his followers one final, solemn warning: "But about that day and hour no one knows, neither the angels of heaven, nor the Son, but only the Father" (Matt. 24:36). "Keep awake therefore, for you do not know on what day your Lord is coming" (Matt. 24:42). The gospels and the creeds remind us to live on tiptoe with joyous anticipation, ready and watching for Christ's appearing.

Prayer:
Maranatha! Our Lord, come!*
Come, for by grace we have received the free gift of salvation from our sin.
Come, for by faith we confess that "Jesus Christ is Lord."
Come, for by scripture we are instructed in righteousness and the will of God.
Come, for by signs and sorrows, your promised coming seems so very near.
Come, Lord Jesus! Blow the trumpet! And gather your elect from around the world. Amen.

* 1 Cor. 16:22.

The Judgment

First Reading: Rom. 2:1–16
Poetry and Wisdom: Ps. 96:1–13
Second Reading: Matt. 25:1–46

"For the Son of Man is to come with his angels in the glory of his Father, and then he will repay everyone for what has been done." (Matt. 16:27)

Apostles' Creed: Jesus Christ … will come again to judge the living and the dead.
Nicene Creed: Jesus Christ … will come again in glory to judge the living and the dead.

Is salvation by faith, by faith alone—*sola fide?* Yes, the apostle Paul wrote correctly, "If you confess with your lips that Jesus is Lord and believe in your heart that God raised him from the dead, you will be saved" (Rom. 10:9; cf. Phil. 2:11). This is a saving, transforming faith—a spiritual birth, the beginning of a new life in Christ Jesus (cf. John 3:3–8). However, Jesus warned everyone that a living faith and true righteousness will bear fruit or good deeds (Matt. 7:20f; Acts 26:20). Therefore, the answer to the initial question may also be "no."

Hear again the words of our Lord Jesus, "Not everyone who says to me, 'Lord, Lord,' will enter the kingdom of heaven, but only the one who does the will of my Father in heaven" (Matt. 7:21). The scriptures consistently warn us that in the Day of Judgment "God will repay according to each one's deeds or works" (e.g., Ps. 62:12; Isa. 59:18; Matt. 12:36f; 16:27; Acts 26:20; Rom. 2:6; 2 Cor. 5:10; Rev. 20:12f). How one builds on the foundation of faith in Christ becomes critical in one's present living and in the Day of Judgment.

It is true that our deeds or works may bring rewards or punishments, benefits or losses, in our present earthly experience, as well as having eternal consequences. Many of the proverbs exalt the value of wisdom, integrity, honesty, discipline, industry, thrift, prosperity, moderation, humility, righteousness, and more. Proverbs 24:12 asks, "Will [God] not repay all according to their deeds?" The implied answer is "Yes."

Jesus declared that we are known by the fruit, the deeds, of our lives in this world as well as in the Day of Judgment (Matt. 7:20; 12:33). The five foolish bridesmaids or virgins were prevented entry into the heavenly wedding of God because of their failure to prepare by engaging in the business of the marketplace (Matt. 25:1–13). They could not benefit from the oil of others—the preparation and deeds of the wise. Thus, there is no treasury of merit or surplus of good deeds created by others from which we can draw in the Day of Judgment.

In the parable of the talents, two of the master's servants were rewarded because they were proven trustworthy in a few things, and for that reason they were given greater responsibilities (Matt. 25:21, 23). The third servant was condemned for his fear and laziness (Matt. 25:26). Two were promoted, and one was fired. This parable provides practical wisdom and a warning to a worker of any age and culture in the present world. On the other hand, the parable applies primarily to the final Day of Judgment. Jesus's parable states that the worthless servant was "thrown into the outer darkness where there will weeping and gnashing of teeth" (Matt. 25:30). Therefore, judgment must be recognized as both present and future, earthly and eternal.

In the parable of the great judgment, all nations—those living and the dead—will be gathered before God, who judges all according to righteousness and equity. His criteria in dividing the sheep from the goats is clear: "Come, you that are blessed by my Father, inherit the kingdom prepared for you from the foundation of the world; for I was hungry and you gave me food, I was thirsty and you gave me something to drink, I was a stranger and you welcomed me, I was naked and you gave me clothing, I was sick and you took care of me, I was in prison and you visited me" (Matt. 25:34–36). This is a social mandate of personal responsibility, for Jesus adds, "Truly I tell you, just as you did it to one of the least of these who are members of my family, you did it to me" (Matt. 25:40).

Prayer (*Collect for Purity* adapted):
Almighty God, to you all hearts are open,
    all desires known, and from you no secrets are hid:
Cleanse the thoughts of our hearts
    by the inspiration of your Holy Spirit,
that we may perfectly love you,
    and worthily magnify your holy Name
    in our living, our death, and the Day of Judgment;
    through Christ our Lord. Amen.

The Kingdom of God

First Reading: 2 Pet. 1:1–11
Poetry and Wisdom: Ps. 145:1–13
Second Reading: John 18:33–37

"Jesus came to Galilee, proclaiming the good news of God, and saying, 'The time is fulfilled, and the kingdom of God has come near; repent, and believe in the good news.'" (Mark 1:14–15)

Apostles' Creed: No parallel
Nicene Creed: And [Christ's] kingdom will have no end.

———————————

Jesus was born in the kingdom of Herod the Great, king of Judea (37–4 BC; Matt. 2:1; Luke 1:5). Following the death of Herod the Great in 4 BC, the kingdom of Judea was ultimately divided into three territories. The southern portion of Palestine became a Roman province ruled by a procurator (e.g., Pilate), while the northern area was divided and ruled by two sons of Herod the Great, that is, Herod Antipas, tetrarch of Galilee, and his brother Herod Philip, tetrarch of the northeast region of Ituraea and Trachonitis (Luke 3:1). All of these regional authorities served by appointment and in submission to the reign of the Roman emperor Tiberius Caesar (Mark 12:14; John 19:12). These were the political territorial kingdoms of Palestine during the adult life of Jesus.

  Americans tend to have vague, romantic views about royalty—kings, queens, princes, and princesses. The majority of modern royalty (e.g., United Kingdom, Belgium, Jordan, Netherlands, Spain, Sweden, et al.) are "constitutional monarchs." That means that their powers are limited and defined by a constitution. Other kings (e.g., Brunei, Oman, Qatar, Saudi Arabia, et al.) are "absolute monarchs." An absolute monarch wields unrestricted political power over the sovereign state and its people, including life and death. In practice, the absolute king may be counterbalanced by political groups, such as the aristocracy and clergy, which certainly affected the trial of Jesus before Pilate, as the leaders called for Jesus's crucifixion.

Ideally, kings, prime ministers, presidents, and parliaments strive to provide security, peace, and tranquility for their people. They administer laws, justice with mercy, equally for the benefit of all, especially caring for the poor and vulnerable subjects within their realm. An ideal king is feared, respected, and loved by his people.

When Jesus proclaimed the "kingdom of God has come near," it was good news to his listeners, who were living in the kingdom of Herod and Caesar. To Herod, "Jesus, the king of the Jews" was a political rival and an alarming threat to his rule (Matt. 2:3f). To the Jerusalem Council, Jesus was worthy of death for blasphemy, a religious charge; however, the accusations they brought in the civil court of Pilate was that Jesus claimed to be "the king of the Jews … perverting our nation, forbidding us to pay taxes to the emperor" (Luke 23:2). Pilate understood a kingdom as political, temporal, and territorial. If true, these allegations brought by the Jewish leaders were treasonous. On the other hand, Jesus's description of his kingdom, the kingdom of God, as "not from this world," rather a kingdom of truth, mystified Pilate (John 18:36–37).

The kingdom of God, Jesus proclaimed, "is not coming with things that can be observed … for [it] is among you" (Luke 17:20f). Where? Look at creation. God is the Lord and sovereign over all creation (Gen. 1:1; 14:18; Ps. 19:1ff; 24:1). The grandeur, beauty, order, infinite design of all creation reveal the eternal power and divine nature of the living God, the Lord and King over all (Rom. 1:20). Creation allows no one an excuse of ignorance. While many search and perhaps grope for God, the Great King and Lord over all creation, others find him, for he is not far from any of us (Acts 17:17).

The kingdom of God is present in the person, ministry, and miracles of Jesus (Matt. 12:28; Lk. 11:20). Jesus exhorts everyone, "Believe in God, believe also in me" (John 14:1; 3:16). Believe in the Lord and King over all, and believe also in the one whom God has sent to remind us of this unchanging, eternal truth, "God loves the world!" Jesus likens himself to the gate (Jn. 10:7, 9; Matt. 7:13–14). Entry, therefore, is conditional, and it demands a personal decision—faith in Jesus Christ (Rom. 10:9). The kingdom of God accepts only volunteers, only believers, although the entrance of some may appear to have elements of a draft or conscription (e.g., Saul/Paul, Acts 9:4–6).

Those who enter and live in this kingdom of our Lord accept his will and word as our constitution of redemption, liberty, and practice. God is our king, and we submit to his authority over our behavior, now and forever. We love him and desire to please him in all that we think, say, and do. As his disciples, we also know that the will and word of God is broadly ignored, belittled, and abused in our present sinful and wicked world. Therefore, Jesus exhorts us to continually pray, "Your kingdom come, your will be done, on earth as it is in heaven" (Matt. 6:10). We pray and work for the realization of God's kingdom now as we anticipate the future glorious invasion and final conquest of all lesser kings by "the King of kings and Lord of lords!" (Rev. 17:14; 19:16; 1 Tim. 6:15).

Prayer:
We bow down in obeisance to you,
  King of kings and Lord of lords.
Like the wise men who knelt in joy and homage
  before the Christ child born in Bethlehem,

We kneel and worship before the crucifix, the cross,
    before the one who suffered in agony on that cross,
    dying in triumph over our enemy, for our peace.
With the saints of the ages, we join the joyous procession,
    shouting, "Hosanna to Jesus Christ our King,
    whose kingdom and reign will have no end." Amen.

The Holy Spirit

First Reading: John 14:15–27; 16:7–15
Poetry and Wisdom: Ps. 48:1–14
Second Reading: Acts 2:1–21

"Jesus said to them again, 'Peace be with you. As the Father has sent me, so I send you.' When he had said this, he breathed on them and said to them, 'Receive the Holy Spirit.'" (John 20:21–22)

Apostles' Creed: I believe in the Holy Spirit.
Nicene Creed: We believe in the Holy Spirit, the Lord.

Christians believe in one God who manifests himself in three *personas* or modes—Father, Son, and Holy Spirit. Each manifestation or revelation is fully and equally God. For this reason, Christians are monotheists and trinitarians, and the ecumenical creeds affirm this essential character of our faith.

Before his ascension, Jesus instructed his disciples "not to leave Jerusalem, but to wait there for the promise of the Father ... '[For] you will be baptized with the Holy Spirit not many days from now'" (Acts 1:4f). The promised gift of the Spirit was experienced ten days after the Lord's ascension and fifty days after the Passover. Pentecost (fiftieth day) was the second of the three major Jewish feasts— Passover, Pentecost, and Tabernacles (Exod. 23:14–17; 34:23; Lev. 23:15f; Deut. 16:9–16). These festivals required a sacred assembly of joy, rejoicing, and thanksgiving before God with offerings. No one was excused, neither a child nor a newly married bride and groom (Deut. 16:11; Joel 2:16).

Pentecost was also known as the Feast of Weeks and the Feast of First Fruits. The feast marked the beginning of wheat harvest, early summer, and the season fit for travel (*Midrash Rabbah*, Song of Songs 7.2). The latter explains the presence of so many devout Jews from the Diaspora—"from every nation under heaven" (Acts 2:5)—being in Jerusalem for Pentecost. Beyond the agricultural significance and presentation of the first fruits of the harvest to God, Pentecost was also a day of celebration and renewal of the covenant, the giving of the Torah or law at Mount Sinai. Therefore, Pentecost celebrated the birthday of Israel (cf. Deut. 4:6–8).

Christians celebrate Pentecost as the birthday of a new covenant, the birthday of a new people of God, the birthday of the church. For it was on this Jewish holiday that 120 followers of Jesus Christ received God's gracious gift, the baptism of the Holy Spirit (Acts 2:1). The prophet Jeremiah foretold the coming of a new covenant with the people of God:

> The days are surely coming, says the Lord, when I will make a new covenant with the house of Israel and the house of Judah. It will not be like the covenant that I made with their ancestors when I took them by the hand to bring them out of the land of Egypt ... But this is the covenant that I will make with the house of Israel after those days, says the Lord: I will put my law within them, and I will write it on their hearts; and I will be their God, and they shall be my people. No longer shall they teach one another, or say to each other, "Know the Lord," for they shall all know me, from the least of them to the greatest, says the Lord." (Jer. 31:31–34; Heb. 8:8–11)

The Holy Spirit is God present and active in the hearts and lives of his people.

Jesus promised his disciples that they would receive the Spirit of truth or Advocate who would be with them forever (John 14:16). The Spirit of God will abide with you, and he will be in you (John 14:17). God, the Holy Spirit, is our teacher, our guide, reminding us of all that Jesus has taught us. The Holy Spirit gives life, joy, and peace with God (John 3:3–8; 14:27).

Prayer:
Blessed Spirit of the living God:
By your power we have been born from above—
    baptized by water and Spirit into the family of God.
You now abide with us, Holy Advocate—
    teaching and guiding us in truth and holiness,
    proving the world wrong about sin, righteousness, and judgment.
Blessed Spirit, gift of God, you are our source
    of peace, joy, wisdom, and hope. Amen.

Week 7.2—Passion Week / Holy Monday

The Spirit Gives Life

First Reading: Joel 2:28–32
Poetry and Wisdom: Ps. 51:1–10, 17
Second Reading: Acts 2:22–42

"Peter said to them, 'Repent, and be baptized every one of you in the name of Jesus Christ so that your sins may be forgiven; and you will receive the gift of the Holy Spirit.'" (Acts 2:38)

Apostles' Creed: I believe in the Holy Spirit.
Nicene Creed: We believe in the Holy Spirit, the Lord, the giver of life.

———————

Throughout the scriptures, spirit (Hebrew, *rûaḥ*; Greek, *pneûma*) can have multiple meanings (i.e., spirit, wind, breath, or soul). The wind makes the trees of the forest sway, and the sound may be heard by the human ear (Gen. 3:8; Isa. 7:2; John 3:8). Breath is the sign of life in humans and animals (Gen. 6:17; 7:22) and is the gift and creation of God (Gen. 6:3; Isa. 42:5). Breath is the basic principle of life, and it departs at the time of one's death (Gen. 1:30; Ps. 78:39; 104:29f; 146:4; Luke 8:55; 23:46; Matt. 27:50). The spirit may also denote the immaterial aspect of one's life (e.g., flesh and spirit). Therefore, spirit may refer to one's personality, feelings, animation, and emotions.

Most occurrences of spirit in both the Old and New Testaments refer to the Spirit of the Lord God. Pharaoh recognized Joseph to be "one in whom is the spirit of God" (Gen. 41:38). In the time of the Judges, "the spirit of the Lord took possession of Gideon," transforming him into a courageous, mighty warrior who led Israel to a miraculous victory over the Midianites (Judg. 6:34). The Lord filled Bezalel "with divine spirit, with skill, intelligence and knowledge in every kind of craft, to devise artistic designs, to work in gold, silver, and bronze, in cutting stones for setting, and in carving wood ... and he has inspired him to teach" (Exod. 35:30–34). The spirit of God gave these gifts for the construction of the tabernacle (Exod. 36:8). King David confessed his sin and pled with God for divine mercy: "Create in me a clean heart, O God, and put a new and right spirit within me. Do not cast me away from your presence, and do not take your holy spirit from me. Restore to me the joy of your salvation" (Ps. 51:10–12).

In the New Testament also, the Spirit of God gives life, courage, and gifts. Jesus explained this new spiritual life to Nicodemus, a teacher of Israel, "Very truly, I tell you, no one can enter the kingdom of God without being born of water and Spirit. What is born of the flesh is flesh, and what is born of the Spirit is spirit" (John 3:5f). Thus, to everyone who believes and receives Jesus Christ as Lord and Savior, the Spirit gives birth to a new creation, a child of God (John 1:12f; 2 Cor. 5:17).

The Acts of the Apostles is the story of the birth of the church on the day of Pentecost, and the chapters that follow tell the continuation of the miraculous story in the lives and activities of the apostles. All of the disciples of Jesus who were assembled in anticipation on Pentecost "were filled with the Holy Spirit" (Acts 2:4). The Spirit gave them the ability to speak in other languages and dialects spoken by the devout Jewish listeners from every nation under heaven who were present in Jerusalem for the holiday (Acts 2:5ff). It may have been a miracle of speaking and/or hearing, for the amazed and perplexed crowd that gathered to witness the Pentecost phenomena exclaimed, "How is it that we hear, each of us, in our own native language?" (Acts 2:8). What were they hearing? Those filled with the Holy Spirit were proclaiming God's deeds of power (Acts 2:11, 22–24, 36).

Peter declared that the miracle of Pentecost was in fulfillment of the words of the prophet Joel: "In the last days it will be, God declares, that I will pour out my Spirit upon all flesh ..." (Acts 2:17–21; Joel 2:28–32). This marks the beginning of a new chapter in the activity of God. Peter proclaimed the divine promise, "Repent, and be baptized every one of you in the name of Jesus Christ so that your sins may be forgiven; and you will receive the gift of the Holy Spirit. For the promise is for you, for your children, and for all who are far away, everyone whom the Lord our God calls to him" (Acts 2:38f).

Prayer:
Blessed Holy Spirit, the giver of life and inspiration:
Your transforming power and presence is observed
    throughout the pages of the sacred scriptures.
Pentecost, however, marks a new beginning,
    the fulfillment of your promised gift,
    poured out upon all flesh;
To everyone who believes in Jesus Christ—
    first- and twenty-first century disciples alike—
Giving life, courage, and confidence
    to proclaim God's deeds of power without bias
    to our community, city, state, nation,
    and to the ends of the earth. Amen.

The Holy Trinity

First Reading: Acts 10:1–48
Poetry and Wisdom: Ps. 100:1–5
Second Reading: Matt. 28:16–20

"Go therefore and make disciples of all nations, baptizing them in the name of the Father and of the Son and of the Holy Spirit, and teaching them to obey everything that I have commanded you. And remember, I am with you always, to the end of the age." (Matt. 28:19–20)

Apostles' Creed: I believe in the Holy Spirit.
Nicene Creed: We believe in the Holy Spirit ... who proceeds from the Father and the Son, who with the Father and the Son is worshipped and glorified.

The Acts of the Apostles tells the story of the church, the activity of the apostles, primarily Peter and Paul, and the revelation of the Holy Spirit in the gospel's advance from Jerusalem to Rome, inclusive of Jews, Samaritans, and Gentiles. The activity of the Holy Spirit is the primary theme in this historical book of the New Testament. In fact, of the ninety-five references to the "Holy Spirit" found in the sixty-six books of the Bible, forty-one appear in the Book of Acts.

In his farewell commission, Jesus promised his apostles, "You will receive power when the Holy Spirit has come upon you; and you will be my witnesses in Jerusalem, in all Judea and Samaria, and to the ends of the earth" (Acts 1:8). Throughout the book, there is a repeated refrain: "They were or he was filled with the Holy Spirit."[1] The presence and activity of the Holy Spirit has some characteristics common to people drunk with wine (Acts 2:13). The apostles did many wonders and signs (Acts 2:43; 3:6), and they had a new boldness in the proclamation of the gospel.[2] The Holy Spirit is God present in "deeds of power."[3]

In the Acts of the Apostles, God the Holy Spirit is sometimes named simply "the Spirit,"[4] and one time he is identified as "the Spirit of Jesus" (Acts 16:7). This illustrates the synonymous terminology that is used in reference to God the Holy Spirit throughout scripture.

Paul the apostle refers to the Holy Spirit using three terms, while referring to one and the same Spirit, "You are not in the flesh; you are in the *Spirit*, since the *Spirit of God* dwells in you. Anyone who does not have the *Spirit of Christ* does not belong to him" (Rom. 8:9). Again, in his First Letter to the Corinthians, Paul refers to the Spirit with similar, interchangeable terminology: "Therefore I want you to understand that no one speaking by the *Spirit of God* ever says 'Let Jesus be cursed!' and no one can say 'Jesus is Lord' except by the *Holy Spirit*. Now there are varieties of gifts, but the *same Spirit*; and there are varieties of services, but the *same Lord*; and there are varieties of activities, but it is the *same God* who activates all of them in everyone" (12:3–6). The source of our Christian diversity of spiritual and natural gifts, the diverse ways our gifts are used in service, and the diverse activities are quite profound and beautiful. The point being that no matter the terminology—Spirit, Lord, or God—the source is one and the same.

Therefore, these studies in the ecumenical creeds have emphasized the unity and oneness of the Lord God—God the Father, God the Son, and God the Spirit—one God in three manifestations, modes, or revelations. When we worship, we worship the one true God. In his response to Satan's third temptation, Jesus declared with finality, "It is written, 'Worship the Lord your God, and serve only him'" (Matt. 4:8–10; cf. Deut. 10:20; 6:13). Whether we pray "Our Father ..." (Matt. 6:9), "in the name of Jesus" (John 14:13f; 16:23; Acts 2:38; Phil. 2:10), or "in the Spirit" (John 4:24; Eph. 6:18; Jude 1:20), our prayers are addressed to the Lord God, the Almighty. The Revelation to John can be summarized by this two-word reminder: "Worship God!" (22:9).

Matthew 28:16–20 is known as our Lord's Great Commission to his disciples and thus his commission to the church. This is the only place in all of scripture where the trinitarian baptismal formula is found: "Go therefore and make disciples of all nations, baptizing them in the name of the Father and of the Son and of the Holy Spirit" (28:19). It is important to note that "the name" is singular, indicating one God in unity and authority who has made himself known to us in three persons—Father, Son, and Holy Spirit. This is not the only baptismal formula found in Christian scriptures and practice, for many were baptized "in the name of Jesus" (Acts 2:38; 8:16; 10:48; 19:5; Rom. 6:3; et al.). The trinitarian formula, however, is most commonly used in the sacrament of baptism from the first century to the present (cf. *Didache* 7:1).[5]

Prayer:
As on the day of Pentecost in Jerusalem, and
Subsequently, to believers in Samaria, Caesarea, and Ephesus,
Pour out the Holy Spirit once more upon your church
That we might make known God's deeds of power and wonder with boldness,
To awaken our cynical, humanistic, and immoral friends and neighbors.
In the name of the Father, the Son, and the Holy Spirit. Amen.

[1] "Filled with /full of the Holy Spirit"—Acts 2:4; 4:8, 31; 6:5; 7:55; 9:17; 11:24; 13:9, 52; cf. 10:44; 11:15.

[2] Apostolic boldness—Acts 4:13, 29, 31; 9:22, 27f; 13:46; 14:3; 18:26, 28; 19:8; 28:31.

[3] "Deeds of power"—Acts 2:11, 22; 4:33; 6:8; 8:19; 9:22; 10:38.

[4] "The Spirit"—Acts 2:4, 17, 18; 6:3, 10; 8:16, 18, 29, 39; 10:19; 11:12, 28; 19:21; 20:22; 21:4.

[5] "In the name of the Father, the Son, and the Holy Spirit," known as the Sign of the Cross, is the verbal and/or the physical gesture of devotion tracing the two lines of the Lord's cross—from the forehead down to the breast and from shoulder to shoulder (left to right). The reminder of the cross of Christ may also be done by the thumb on the forehead.

The Spirit and the Prophets

First Reading: Acts 3:17–26
Poetry and Wisdom: Prov. 29:18
Second Reading: Eph. 4:1–16

"Long ago God spoke to our ancestors in many and various ways by the prophets, but in these last days he has spoken to us by a Son." (Heb. 1:1)

Apostles' Creed: I believe in the Holy Spirit.
Nicene Creed: We believe in the Holy Spirit … who has spoken through the prophets.

The Holy Spirit spoke through the prophets in ancient times, and he continues to speak through his prophets to this day (Heb. 1:1). This certainly expands the meaning of the creed beyond an affirmation of the prophets of the Old Testament (e.g., Elijah, Elisha, Isaiah, Jeremiah, Ezekiel, et al.). What or who then is a prophet? A prophet or prophetess is an individual called by God and authorized to communicate the divine message to an individual or people. The scriptures help us to understand what is meant by the word "prophet."

The definition of a prophet is found in Exodus 7:1–2: "The Lord said to Moses, 'See, I have made you like God to Pharaoh, and your brother Aaron shall be your prophet. You shall speak all that I command you, and your brother Aaron shall tell Pharaoh to let the Israelites go out of his land.'" Aaron declared God's word, which was given to Moses. The role of the prophet is also described in Numbers 12:6: "When there are prophets among you, I the Lord make myself known to them in visions; I speak to them in dreams." Although a prophet's message may forewarn of future consequences of sins and transgressions or promises of blessings, restoration, and hope; however, foretelling the future is not the primary purpose of a prophet. The prophet is a messenger, a preacher of divine truth, a spokesperson for God.

The prophet Isaiah was such a man on a mission for God: "The spirit of the Lord God is upon me, because the Lord has anointed me; he has sent me to bring good news to the oppressed, to bind up the brokenhearted, to proclaim liberty to the captives, and release to the prisoners; to proclaim the year of the Lord's favor" (Isa. 61:1f). He called for a renewal of righteousness and justice in Jerusalem and Judah, reassuring the faithful of divine blessing and warning the faithless of God's certain punishment. Jesus reaffirmed the divine mission seven hundred years later by quoting these words of the prophet Isaiah (cf. Luke 4:18f).

The histories of Elijah (1 Kings 17:1ff), Elisha (2 Kings 2:13ff), and the literary prophecies of Isaiah, Jeremiah, and Ezekiel repeat well-known phrases such as "hear the word of the Lord," "the Lord said," "thus says the Lord the God of Israel," and other similar references to the source and authority of their divine message. The source and authority of the prophets in the twenty-first century is the written word of God—that is, "according to the scripture," "the Bible says," or "Jesus said." The prophets speak as the mouthpiece and voice of God. They declare the word of God.

Most appropriately, Jesus was the greatest of all the prophets, and he is given the title several times.* Jesus Christ was, and is, God's messenger and message of salvation as attested by God with deeds of power, wonders, and signs (Acts 3:22). He was crucified and killed, but God raised him up from the dead. Jesus is God's prophet, God's word to the world (John 1:1).

God continues to speak through his people and prophets to this day. Jesus promised that after his death, resurrection, and ascension, the Holy Spirit would be given to his disciples (John 14:16f, 26; 16:7–11). The Holy Spirit is God present and active in the life of every believer (John 14:17). Jesus refers to the Spirit as our *Paraclete* or Advocate (John 14:16). The Greek technical term refers to one who is called or appointed to come "alongside" us like a lawyer to give wise counsel, to teach and guide into the truth, and to glorify Jesus Christ (John 16:13–15). The Holy Spirit is God with us, with all believers. Therefore, Pentecost is the watershed commencing a new era of prophecy. The Spirit inspires us all to know and proclaim the word of God by our word and witness.

After Pentecost, the classic, vocational definition of a prophet still persists. A prophet or prophetess is an individual called by God and authorized to communicate his divine message. In the Acts of the Apostles, we read, "Now in the church at Antioch there were prophets and teachers: Barnabas … and Saul. While they were worshiping the Lord and fasting, the Holy Spirit said, 'Set apart for me Barnabas and Saul for the work to which I have called them'" (13:1–2).

In the modern Christian community, a prophet or prophetess may be known by many other titles (e.g., priest, pastor, bishop, apostle, missionary, evangelist, teacher, elder, deacon, et al.) (cf. Acts 14:23; 1 Cor. 12:28; Eph. 4:11–14; 1 Tim. 5:17). He or she is a respected person in the community, full of the Spirit, known for wisdom, and called by God to holy office and leadership (cf. Acts 6:3). The church confirms God's call and gifts by ordination, the rite of the laying on of hands (Acts 6:6; 13:3; 1 Tim. 4:14). It is vitally important that we listen attentively to our contemporary prophets and thus hear the word of the Lord.

Prayer:
Blessed Spirit of God, come in your fullness,
Teaching us the truth about sin, righteousness, and judgment,
Inspiring in us a prophetic voice and boldness in the world,
Proclaiming all that Jesus said and did by our word and witness,
Living in love, unity, and peace with God and neighbor. Amen.

* Matt. 21:11, 46; Luke 7:16; 24:19; John 4:19; 6:14; 7:40; 9:17.

The Church of God

First Reading: John 17:13–24
Poetry and Wisdom: Ps. 133:1–3
Second Reading: Matt. 16:13–20

"You are Peter, and on this rock I will build my church, and the gates of Hades will not prevail against it." (Matt. 16:18)

Apostles' Creed: I believe in ... the holy catholic church, the communion of saints.
Nicene Creed: We believe in one holy catholic and apostolic church.

The "church" (Greek: *ekklēsia*) appears only three times in the gospels and only in Matthew (16:18; 18:17[2t]). However, it appears 111 times elsewhere in the New Testament. Sometimes it refers to a Christian assembly or congregation meeting together in a specific house (Rom. 16:5) or city (Acts 11:22). At other times, it may refer to all the Christians living in a city or region (Acts 5:11; 9:31; Phil. 4:15; 1 Thess. 1:1). In the ecumenical creeds, the church is a universal, comprehensive term, inclusive of all believers in Jesus Christ (1 Cor. 12:28; Eph. 1:22; 3:10, 21; Col. 1:24).

According to the scriptures and succinctly stated in the creeds, the church of God is distinguished and known by four marks, attributes, or characteristics: one, holy, catholic, and apostolic. Let us consider these "four marks of the church" one by one.

First Mark—One

"I ask ... that they may all be one ... so that the
world may believe." (John 17:20–21)

It is quite fitting on Maundy Thursday to recall the Last Supper
and our Lord's command: "I give you a new commandment, that
you love one another. Just as I have loved you, you also should love
one another. By this everyone will know that you are my disciples,
if you have love for one another" (John 13:34–35). The command
for love and unity continues in Jesus's high priestly prayer for his
disciples in the waning hours prior to his arrest, trial, and crucifixion:
"I ask ... that they may all be one ... so that the world may believe."
(John 17:20–21)

The Acts of the Apostles is a narrative of unity, explosive growth,
cultural and ethnic diversity, and the progressively difficult challenge
to sustain the unity of the church. On the day of Pentecost as many as
three thousand Jews and proselytes from Jerusalem, Judea, Samaria,
and more than a dozen countries responded to Peter's exhortation to
repent and be baptized (Acts 2:5–13, 38–41). Although they were all
Jews or proselytes to Judaism, cultural diversity begins to affect the
young church. Initially, they were one: "They devoted themselves to
the apostles' teaching and fellowship, to the breaking of bread and
the prayers ... All who believed were together and had all things in
common" (Acts 2:42–44). In Acts 4:4, another five thousand Jews
of Jerusalem believed in Jesus the Messiah and were added to the
church (cf. 5:14). Some were traditional Hebrews, while others were
more liberal, modern, Hellenistic Jews, creating a significant stress
to the unity of the church (cf. 6:1, 7).

The challenge increases further with the addition of believers
in Samaria (Acts 8:4–8), the Gentile centurion Cornelius and his
household (Acts 10:44–48), the Hellenistic Gentiles of Antioch
(Acts 11:19–21), and the diverse circumcised and uncircumcised
believers in Galatia and Asia Minor (Acts 12:24; 13:48f; 14:1, 21).
The problem of unity with diversity simmers and boils to a crisis in

Acts 15. At the Jerusalem conference, the leaders—Peter, Barnabas, Paul, James, and others—and the church unanimously agreed to four essential principles (cf. Acts 15:20, 29). The four can be summarized into two: Gentile believers are not required to convert to Judaism, and all believers are to abstain from sexual immorality. All believers are one in Jesus Christ and activated by the same Spirit but diverse in language, ethnicity, culture, history, and traditions.

Second Mark—Holy
"You shall be holy, for I am holy." (Lev. 11:45; 1 Pet. 1:16)

What does it mean when the church joins with the angels of heaven in praise, singing, "Holy, holy, holy, the Lord God the Almighty" (Rev. 4:8; Isa. 6:3)? God is holy, creator, perfect, power, majesty, righteous, just, trustworthy, morally pure, steadfast love, and mercy. Holy and holiness implies that which is associated with heaven, the divine, the sacred, and thus a separation from the profane (i.e., human infirmity, impurity, and sin). And yet these attributes fail to fully comprehend the nature and character of God. He is spirit and remains a mystery. Therefore we worship him in awe, with reverent respect and with a healthy fear.

The scriptures narrate the story of a holy God on a quest to redeem and create a holy people (Exod. 19:5f; Lev. 11:44f; Isa. 62:12; 1 Pet. 2:9f). The church is God's holy people, a holy nation, the children and family of the living God (Mark 3:34f; John 1:12f; Rom. 9:26; Gal. 6:10; 1 Pet. 2:4–10; Rev. 7:4, 9). The people of God are called "saints," which means "the holy ones" (Acts 9:13, 32; Rom. 8:27; 12:13; 15:25; 1 Cor. 6:1f). In fact, "saints" is synonymous and used interchangeably with "church" in the New Testament (2 Cor. 1:1; Eph. 2:19; Col. 1:4).

Born of the Spirit (John 3:8; 2 Cor. 5:17), the church is sanctified and made holy by the word and work of God (John 17:17). The church—individually and as a body of believers—increasingly reveals the nature and character of a holy God. She consists of a people transformed from the inside out by the power of God, not the other way around. Jesus declared, "It is from within, from the human heart, that evil intentions come: fornication, theft, murder, adultery, avarice, wickedness, deceit, licentiousness, envy, slander, pride, folly. All these evil things come from within, and they defile a person" (Mark 7:21–23; cf. Gal. 5:19–21). "By contrast, the fruit of the Spirit is love, joy, peace, patience, kindness, generosity, faithfulness, gentleness, and self-control" (Gal. 5:22–23). These are the characteristics of the holy people of God, both present in some measure and progressively so to spiritual maturity. The church is God's living witness in the world but not of it (John 17:14–16).

Third Mark—Catholic
"There is no longer Jew or Greek, there is no longer
slave or free, there is no longer male and female; for
all of you are one in Christ Jesus." (Gal. 3:28)

"Catholic" means the church universal, comprehensive, inclusive, and undivided. Christ came to create one new humanity and peace in the household of God, breaking down the dividing walls (Eph. 2:11–22). "There is no longer Jew or Greek, there is no longer slave or free, there is no longer male and female; for all of you are one in Christ Jesus" (Gal. 3:28). To these sources of division—ethnic, social, and gender walls—it may be appropriate to add an economic divide (i.e., "rich or poor"), a cultural divide (i.e., educated or uneducated), a language divide (i.e., English or Spanish), and still others.

In Paul's letter to the Corinthians, he responds to reports of quarrels and loyalties that are dividing the church. Some were saying, "I belong to Paul," or "I belong to Apollos," or "I belong to Cephas," or "I belong to Christ" (1 Cor. 1:12). That is similar to saying, "I belong to the Roman Catholic Church," or "I belong to the Orthodox Church," or "I belong to the Anglican Church," or "I am a Protestant," or "I am an Evangelical." Still other names of loyalty and traditions may be added. "Has Christ been divided?" Paul asks (1 Cor. 1:13). The question implies the simple answer, "No!" The church of God, the body of Christ, is bigger and broader than any subdivision or sectarian tradition. Christ was crucified and died for everyone who believes in him.

The creeds remind us of that essential, inclusive unity of all believers in Christ Jesus. In God's revelation to the apostle John, John sees an illuminating vision of the church: "I looked, and there was a great multitude that no one could count, from every nation, from all tribes and peoples and languages, standing before the throne and before the Lamb, robed in white" (Rev. 7:9). Regardless of our present, earthly tradition or liturgy of worship, all who believe are members of Christ's body, "the one holy catholic and apostolic church."

Fourth Mark—Apostolic
"You are citizens with the saints and also members
of the household of God, built upon the foundation
of the apostles and prophets, with Christ Jesus
himself as the cornerstone." (Eph. 2:19–20)

The preeminence of Peter among the twelve apostles appears to all readers of the gospels and the history of the early church. Peter was the first called (Mark 1:16; Luke 5:8–10), first to confess faith in Jesus the Messiah (Mark 8:29), first to see the risen Christ (Luke 24:12, 34), commissioned to feed God's sheep (John 21:15–19), the recognized leader of the 120 disciples in the upper room (Acts 1:15), and God's apostolic spokesman to the world on Pentecost (Acts 2:14–41). Boldly Peter condemned the Jewish leaders for their rejection and crucifixion of Jesus the Messiah (3:12–16; 4:8–12, 19–20). God's choice and appointment of Simon Peter as "the rock" upon which he would build his church is repeatedly confirmed in God's unfolding story (Matt. 16:18; Acts 8:14–17; 10:44–48; 15:7).

At the conclusion of Peter's sermon on Pentecost, thousands of new believers "devoted themselves to the apostles' teaching ..."

(Acts 2:41–42). There was recognition that the apostles were their key, their link and connection, to knowing Jesus Christ. The apostles were those chosen by Jesus, to be with him, to witness his miracles, to hear his words, and to follow him to the cross. Yes, they were slow to understand. Yes, Jesus rebuked and condemned their unbelief. Yes, they faltered, failed, and fled at the crucial hour. And, yes, also, Jesus commissioned the apostles to tell the good news of God to all nations (Matt. 28:19f).

The bedrock and foundation on which God has built his church is much greater than Peter. The foundation of the apostles and prophets includes the Twelve (Acts 1:13, 26), Barnabas (Acts 4:36; 13:1), the seven deacons (Acts 6:5f), Saul/Paul (Acts 9:15; 13:2), James (Acts 12:17; 15:13), Priscilla (Acts 18:26), and many others who had a close connection with the living and risen Christ (Acts 1:14; 13:1). This esteemed, apostolic cadre of men and women practiced, proclaimed, and preserved the story of Jesus—at first orally and then in the written gospels, history, and letters circulated for evangelism, teaching, and nurturing the church.

The apostolic foundation has preserved the truth of God in Christ and safeguarded the church from the intrusion of false and extraneous teachings and practices through the centuries.

Prayer:
We love your church, O Lord:
> Assembled in worship and dispersed in vocation and service,
> A communion of saints and a salty witness in the world.

We love your church, O Lord:
> Your family, your flock, your fruitful vine with many branches,
> Your body, your bride, for whom you suffered, bled, and died.

We love your church, O Lord:
> The one, holy, catholic, and apostolic church,
> A great multitude that no one can count
> From every nation, tribe, people, and language. Amen.

Baptism and the Forgiveness of Sins

First Reading: Rom. 6:1–11
Poetry and Wisdom: Ps. 130:1–6
Second Reading: John 1:19–34

"Thus it is written, that the Messiah is to suffer and to rise from the dead on the third day, and that repentance and forgiveness of sins is to be proclaimed in his name to all nations, beginning from Jerusalem." (Luke 24:46–47)

Apostles' Creed: We believe in ... the forgiveness of sins.
Nicene Creed: We acknowledge one baptism for the forgiveness of sins.

Jesus Christ suffered, died, and was buried on Good Friday, the Jewish Day of Preparation for the Passover (Mark 15:42; John 19:14, 31, 42). At about three in the afternoon (Mark 15:34), the appointed hour for the priests to kill the lambs for the evening Passover meal, Jesus breathed his last (Mark 15:37). Remember John the Baptist's introduction of Jesus to his disciples: "Here is the Lamb of God who takes away the sin of the world!" (John 1:29, 36).

The forgiveness of our sins is the good news of God proclaimed by the cross. This is our message and declaration to the world (Luke 24:46). We humbly kneel at the cross and remember the new covenant sealed by our Lord's blood. Remember Jesus's words at the Last Supper: "He took a cup, and after giving thanks he gave it to them, saying, 'Drink from it, all of you; for this is my blood of the covenant, which is poured out for many for the forgiveness of sins'" (Matt. 26:27–28). Yes, we remember! Yes, we believe in Christ for the forgiveness of our sins! And yes, we proclaim the good news in our exalted Savior's name to all nations: "Repent, believe, and receive God's forgiveness for your sins!" (cf. Acts 10:43; 13:38–39; Heb. 6:1–2; 9:22).

The Epistle to the Hebrews exhorts us to "go on toward perfection, leaving behind the basic teaching about Christ, and not laying again the foundation: *repentance* from dead works and *faith* toward God, instruction about *baptisms*, laying on of hands, resurrection of the dead, and eternal judgment" (Heb. 6:1–2, italics mine). Again, the Nicene Creed reminds us of the basic teaching about Christ and the significance of Christian baptism. It appears that the Church Fathers had Paul's creedal summary in mind when they added "one baptism" to the Apostles' Creed: "There is one body and one Spirit, just as you were called to the one hope of your calling, one Lord, one faith, one baptism, one God and Father of all, who is above all and through all and in all" (Eph. 4:4–5).

Baptism certainly has multiple meanings in the scriptures. Jesus referred to his imminent crucifixion, death, and burial as his baptism (Mark 10:38–39; Luke 12:50). Paul assumes that all Christians will be familiar with some form of a Christian initiation ritual of baptism (Rom. 6:3). Paul's meaning here, however, remains somewhat unclear. Does his metaphor refer to the act of baptism with water and all its sacramental significance (John 3:22, 26; Acts 2:38, 41; 8:12; 9:18; 10:47; 1 Pet. 3:21)? Or is he referring to a baptism of the Spirit (Matt. 3:11; Mark 1:8; Luke 3:16; John 3:34; Acts 1:5; 11:16; 1 Cor. 12:13; Col. 2:11–12)?

On the other hand, the larger context of Romans 6 helps to clarify Paul's metaphor. Baptism with either water or the Holy Spirit marks a crucial watershed in the life of the Christian. Figuratively, we have become united with Christ in his baptism—participants in his death, burial, and resurrection. "For if we have been united with him in a death like his," Paul writes, "we will certainly be united with him in a resurrection like his" (Rom. 6:5). This is the message of Good Friday and Easter. With Christ we have died to sin, and God has raised us to live a new life.

The sacrament of baptism with water is a public confession before the church that we have indeed passed from death to newness of life in Christ. The mode of the baptism may be an immersion, a pouring, or a sprinkling of water in the name of the Father, the Son, and the Holy Spirit (*Didache* 7:1–4; Matt. 28:19). In that Christian baptism has replaced the Jewish circumcision of the males at eight days of age (e.g., Luke 2:21), both infant boys and girls and adult men and women equally have been baptized into Christ throughout church history (Acts 10:47; 11:14; 16:14f; 16:31–33; 18:8). They are equally members of the divine covenant and community of faith (Matt. 19:13–15; Mark 10:13–16; Luke 18:15–17).

Just as the Jewish ritual of circumcision was done only once and not repeated, so also, "We acknowledge one baptism for the forgiveness of sins." Yes, there may be an additional ritual of confirmation (maturity), the laying on of hands in ordination of a priest or elder, or the appointment to another office in the church. However there is only one baptism. All who believe are equal recipients of God's forgiveness of sins.

Prayer:
Gory Golgotha—the scene of our Savior's suffering, shame, and
    death—seems all so evil, a tragic injustice, a sad day of darkness.
And yet all who believe in Jesus Christ, the Lamb of God, call this
    Good Friday, God's day of salvation for all who believe, our
    Passover, our exodus, our day of freedom and the forgiveness
    of sins.
We remember and celebrate our baptism in his name, a baptism of
    death, burial, and resurrection to live a transformed life. Amen.

Week 7.7—Passion Week / Holy Saturday

Resurrection and Eternal Life

First Reading: 1 Cor. 15:12–23
Poetry and Wisdom: Job 19:13–27
Second Reading: John 5:24–29

"For God so loved the world that he gave his only Son, so that everyone who believes in him may not perish but may have eternal life." (John 3:16)

Apostles' Creed: I believe in … the resurrection of the body, and the life everlasting. Amen.
Nicene Creed: We look for the resurrection of the dead, and the life of the world to come. Amen.

―――――――――――

Since medieval times, Christians have assembled after sunset on Good Friday for Tenebrae, which is a solemn worship service of "darkness" or "shadows." The worship consists of scripture readings, hymns, and meditations tracing the story of Christ's passion and death. Systematically the lights in the room are extinguished, and only the Christ candle remains to flicker faintly behind or under the altar table. The people depart in darkness and silence.

The Tenebrae pageantry illustrates the last line of the ecumenical creeds. "I believe in the resurrection … and the life everlasting," as stated in the Apostles' Creed, is changed to, "We look for the resurrection … and the life …" in the Nicene Creed. The phrase is changed from a "confession" to one of anticipation, expectation, and hope. The Tenebrae worshiper anticipates a brighter day, resurrection morning, when the stone will be rolled away and the tomb will be empty. On Easter Sunday, the Christ candle no longer remains hidden but exalted and burning brightly for all the world to see. The last line of the Nicene Creed creates a picture of Christians standing on tiptoe looking for the resurrection and our future, eternal life with God.

A second change made by the Nicene Creed should also be noted. Our future hope is not one of longevity but rather one of quality—life with God in the coming era (Rev. 21:1–4). The scriptures clearly state that on the day of the resurrection all nations, all people who have ever lived, will be assembled before God, our judge (Matt. 25:31–46). It will be a day of separation, "as a shepherd separates the sheep from the goats" (Matt. 25:33). To those on his right, God will say, "Come, you that are blessed by my Father, inherit the kingdom prepared for you from the foundation of the world" (Matt. 25:34). But to those on his left, his judgment is final, "You that are accursed, depart from me into the eternal fire prepared for the devil and his angels" (Matt. 25:41). By what criteria will the determination be made? Have you fed the hungry? Given shelter to the homeless stranger? Clothed the naked? Cared for the sick? And visited those in prison? (Matt. 25:35–36; 42–43). God's judgment will be determined according to what we have done (Rev. 20:12).

The basis of divine judgment should be clear to all. Jesus said, "Do not be astonished at this; for the hour is coming when all who are in their graves will hear his voice and will come out—those who have done good, to the resurrection of life, and those who have done evil, to the resurrection of condemnation" (John 5:28–29). This present time reveals God's "kindness and forbearance and patience" and his desire that everyone would believe and repent (Rom. 2:4). But the day of judgment is coming, Paul warns, when God "will repay according to each one's deeds: to those who by patiently doing good seek for glory and honor and immortality, he will give eternal life; while for those who are self-seeking and who obey not the truth but wickedness, there will be wrath and fury" (Rom 2:6–8).*

On this Holy Saturday, we are prepared to shout to the world, "Christ has been raised from the dead, the first fruits of those who have died" (1 Cor. 15:20). Because he lives, "We look for the resurrection of the dead, and the life of the world to come." Jesus destroyed death and the fear of the grave (1 Cor. 15:26, 55–57). Because he lives, we anticipate tomorrow.

Amen. So let it be! On this rock we stand!

Prayer:
Blessed risen Lord, the first fruits of all who have died:
The rock-hewn tomb was only a temporary residence
    for the physical, perishable body of ash, dust, and earth;
For that which was sown in death was raised
    imperishable and transformed, spiritual and immortal.
Your many resurrection appearances to the perplexed disciples
    create wonder and the assurance of our own eternal hope. Amen.

---

* Additional references concerning the basis of God's judgment, which nullifies "easy believism" and "cheap grace"—Psalm 62:12; Proverbs 24:12; Isaiah 59:18; Jeremiah 17:10; 18:30; Ezekiel 24:14; 33:20; Hosea 12:2; 4:9; Matthew 24:45–25:46; John 5:29; Acts 26:20; Romans 2:6, 10; 1 Corinthians 1:8; 3:12–15; 4:4f; 2 Corinthians 5:10; Galatians 5:14; Ephesians 2:10; 1 Thessalonians 3:13; 5:23; 1 Peter 1:17; 2:12; Revelation 20:12–13.

Section 6

SPRINGTIME FOR THE SOUL

CHRIST IS RISEN!
HALLELUJAH!

Week 8.1—Easter / Resurrection Sunday

Christ Is Risen! Hallelujah!

First Reading: Gen. 2:4–9, 15–17
Poetry and Wisdom: Ps. 111:1–10
Second Reading: Mark 16:1–8; 1:1–15*

"The beginning of the good news of Jesus Christ, the Son of God." (Mark 1:1)

———————

"Christ is risen!" "He is risen indeed!" The Easter acclamation inspires us who believe in our crucified, dead, buried, and risen Lord. We worship him, and yet, like his inner circle of disciples, some doubts may linger (Matt. 28:17).

According to the Gospel of Mark, Mary Magdalene, Mary the mother of James, and Salome entered the empty tomb, where they were met by an angel. He said to them, "Do not be alarmed; you are looking for Jesus of Nazareth, who was crucified. He has been raised; he is not here. Look, there is the place they laid him. But go, tell his disciples and Peter that he is going ahead of you to Galilee; there you will see him, just as he told you" (Mark 16:6–7). The women were seized with such terror and amazement that they fled the tomb and did not know what to do. So they said and did nothing, keeping the good news to themselves.

Apparently, many have considered Mark the "unfinished gospel." Therefore they have added endings following the traditional, abrupt close, which were not in the original text of Mark. Several of those additions to Mark may appear in your biblical text following 16:8. It is in these supplementary sections that some believers find a spurious basis for various signs or proofs of spirituality, especially handling poisonous snakes and drinking deadly poisons. These heretical activities remind us of Jesus's response to the devil, "Do not put the Lord your God to the test" (Luke 4:12; Deut. 6:16).

I believe that Mark intended to end his gospel at 16:8. What was his point? He knew that his disciples were bewildered and troubled with the ending of Jesus's story with an empty tomb. They had many unanswered questions. Where may the disciples find the answers? Go back to the beginning—to the beginning of the gospel story in Galilee. Reread this gospel, and your faith will find new understanding and confidence. Listen again to the words of the angel to the women: "Go, tell his disciples and Peter that he is going ahead of you to Galilee; there you will see him, just as he told you" (Mark 16:7).

The scripture readings today take us back to the beginning—to the beginning of creation in the Garden of Eden and the idyllic design of our Creator. We visualize an environmental sanctity and a profound earthly harmony. Here, we discover a longing for the restoration of a former lost relationship with our Creator.

The Gospel of Mark proclaims the solution, our salvation from sin, our Savior. Mark's opening words lay the one and only foundation for our faith: "The beginning of the good news of Jesus Christ, the Son of God" (1:1). This is the essential starting point of our faith journey. Jesus was, and is, the Son of God. Yes, he did many marvelous miracles and taught us by word and deed how to live in a restored relationship with God.

Prayer:
Holy Father,
We have revisited the tomb and found it empty.
However, our amazement must not end with doubts, fears, and silence.
Rather, we return to the beginning and reaffirm our faith in Jesus Christ,
The Son of God, the foundation on which we build our lives. Amen.

* Gospel parallels: Matt. 28:1–10; 3:1–6, 11–17; 4:1–17; Luke 24:1–11; 3:1–6, 15–18, 21–22; 4:1–15; John 20:1–10.

Lectionary

A Complete List of the Daily Bible Readings for Lent

Section 1—The Foundation of a Living Faith

Week 1.1—Ash Wednesday

Title:	"Springtime for the Soul"
First Reading:	2 Pet. 1:1–15; 3:1–2
Poetry and Wisdom:	Ps. 103:1–14
Second Reading:	Luke 24:1–12
Text:	Luke 24:6–7—"Remember how he told you, while he was still in Galilee, that the Son of Man must be handed over to sinners, and be crucified, and on the third day rise again."

Week 1.2—Thursday

Title:	"The Tree of Life"
First Reading:	Gen. 3:1–24
Poetry and Wisdom:	Prov. 3:13–18
Second Reading:	Rev. 2:7; 21:1–5, 22–27; 22:1–5, 12–14
Text:	Rev. 22:14—"Blessed are those who wash their robes, so that they will have the right to the tree of life and may enter the city by the gates."

Week 1.3—Friday

Title:	"God's Covenant of Faith"
First Reading:	Gen. 17:1–8; 15:6
Poetry and Wisdom:	Ps. 105:1–11
Second Reading:	Luke 1:46–55, 67–75
Text:	Gen. 15:6—"Abram believed the Lord; and the Lord reckoned it to him as righteousness."

Week 1.4—Saturday

Title: "Choose Life!"

First Reading: Deut. 30:6–20; Josh. 24:1–2, 13–15

Poetry and Wisdom: Ps. 16:1–11

Second Reading: Luke 9:57–62; 14:25–35

Text: Luke 9:23—"If any want to become my followers, let them deny themselves and take up their cross daily and follow me."

Week 2.1—Sunday

Title: "A True Disciple"

First Reading: Deut. 4:1–14

Poetry and Wisdom: Ps. 119:1–16

Second Reading: Matt. 5:17–20; 7:21–27

Text: Matt. 7:21—"Not everyone who says to me, 'Lord, Lord,' will enter the kingdom of heaven, but only the one who does the will of my Father in heaven."

Section 2—The Ten Commandments

Week 2.2—Monday

Title: "The Ten Commandments"

First Reading: Exod. 20:1–17

Poetry and Wisdom: Ps. 119:33–48

Second Reading: Matt. 19:16–23

Text: Exod. 31:18—"When God finished speaking with Moses on Mount Sinai, he gave him the two tablets of the covenant, tablets of stone, written with the finger of God."

Week 2.3—Tuesday

Title: "The First Commandment"

First Reading: Exod. 20:1–3; Deut. 6:1–9

Poetry and Wisdom: Ps. 78:1–8

Second Reading: Mark 12:28–34

Text: Exod. 20:3—"You shall have no other gods before me."

Week 2.4—Wednesday

Title: "The Second Commandment"

First Reading: Exod. 20:4–6; Deut. 4:12

Poetry and Wisdom:	Ps. 97:1–12
Second Reading:	John 4:1–26
Text:	Exod. 20:4—"You shall not make for yourself an idol."

Week 2.5—Thursday

Title:	"The Third Commandment"
First Reading:	Exod. 3:1–22; 20:7
Poetry and Wisdom:	Ps. 113:1–9
Second Reading:	Mark 3:20–35
Text:	Exod. 20:7—"You shall not make wrongful use of the name of the Lord your God."

Week 2.6—Friday

Title:	"The Fourth Commandment"
First Reading:	Gen. 2:1–3; Exod. 20:8–11; Deut. 5:12–15
Poetry and Wisdom:	Ps. 84:1–12
Second Reading:	Mark 2:23–28; 3:1–6
Text:	Exod. 20:8—"Remember the Sabbath day, and keep it holy."

Week 2.7—Saturday

Title:	"The Fifth Commandment"
First Reading:	Exod. 20:12; Lev. 19:1–3; Deut. 5:16
Poetry and Wisdom:	Prov. 1:7–8; 10:1; 17:6; 20:20
Second Reading:	Mark 7:1–23
Text:	Exod. 20:12—"Honor your father and your mother."

Week 3.1—Sunday

Title:	"The Sixth Commandment"
First Reading:	Exod. 20:13; 21:12–14; Num. 35:16–30
Poetry and Wisdom:	Ps. 69:1–20
Second Reading:	Matt. 5:17–26
Text:	Exod. 20:13—"You shall not murder."

Week 3.2—Monday

Title:	"The Seventh Commandment"
First Reading:	Exod. 20:14; Lev. 20:10–16
Poetry and Wisdom:	Prov. 6:20–35

Second Reading:	Matt. 5:27–37 [John 8:1–11]
Text:	Exod. 20:14—"You shall not commit adultery."

Week 3.3—Tuesday

Title:	"The Eighth Commandment"
First Reading:	Exod. 20:15; 22:1–15
Poetry and Wisdom:	Prov. 30:1–9
Second Reading:	Luke 3:1–14
Text:	Exod. 20:15—"You shall not steal."

Week 3.4—Wednesday

Title:	"The Ninth Commandment"
First Reading:	Exod. 20:16; 23:1–3; Deut. 19:15–21
Poetry and Wisdom:	Ps. 52:1–9
Second Reading:	Matt. 5:33–37
Text:	Exod. 20:16—"You shall not bear false witness."

Week 3.5—Thursday

Title:	"The Tenth Commandment"
First Reading:	Exod. 20:17
Poetry and Wisdom:	Ps. 112:1–10; Prov. 21:26
Second Reading:	Matt. 16:24–26
Text:	Exod. 20:17—"You shall not covet."

Week 3.6—Friday

Title:	"The Great Commandments"
First Reading:	Deut. 6:1–9; 10:12–13; 11:1; Lev. 19:11–18
Poetry and Wisdom:	Ps. 1:1–6
Second Reading:	Mark 12:28–34
Text:	Luke 10:27—"You shall love the Lord your God with all your heart, and with all your soul, and with all your strength, and with all your mind; and your neighbor as yourself."

Section 3—The Canon of the Christian Faith

Week 3.7—Saturday

Title:	"The Truth of God"
First Reading:	Deut. 8:1–10
Poetry and Wisdom:	Prov. 2:1–11; 3:13–18
Second Reading:	John 18:33–38; 19:16–22
Text:	John 18:38—"Pilate asked Jesus, 'What is truth?'"

Week 4.1—Sunday

Title:	"The Word of God: Old Testament"
First Reading:	Deut. 4:1–8
Poetry and Wisdom:	Ps. 33:1–12
Second Reading:	Luke 16:16–31
Text	Luke 16:31—"If they do not listen to Moses and the prophets, neither will they be convinced even if someone rises from the dead."

Week 4.2—Monday

Title:	"The Word of God: New Testament"
First Reading:	Luke 1:1–4; John 20:30–31; 21:24–25
Poetry and Wisdom:	Ps. 40:1–8
Second Reading:	Acts 2:42; 2 Peter 1:12–14, 20–21; 3:1–2, 14–18
Text	Eph. 2:19–20—"So then you are no longer strangers and aliens, but you are citizens with the saints and also members of the household of God, built upon the foundation of the apostles and prophets, with Christ Jesus himself as the cornerstone."

Section 4—The Lord's Prayer

Week 4.3—Tuesday

Title:	"Jesus Prayed"
First Reading:	Matt. 6:1, 5–8
Poetry and Wisdom:	Ps. 86:1–11
Second Reading:	Luke 18:1–14
Text:	Luke 5:16—"Jesus often withdrew to lonely places and prayed" (NIV).

Title:	"Jesus Teaches Us How to Pray" (Part I)
First Reading:	Luke 11:1–13
Poetry and Wisdom:	Ps. 8:1–9
Second Reading:	Matt. 6:9–15
Text:	Matt. 6:9–10—"Pray then in this way: Our Father in heaven, hallowed be your name. Your kingdom come. Your will be done, on earth as it is in heaven."

Week 4.5—Thursday

Title:	"Jesus Teaches Us How to Pray" (Part II)
First Reading:	Matt. 6:19–34
Poetry and Wisdom:	Ps. 32:1–11
Second Reading:	Matt. 18:21–35
Text:	Matt. 6:11–13—"Pray then in this way … Give us this day our daily bread. And forgive us our debts, as we also have forgiven our debtors. And do not bring us to the time of trial, but rescue us from the evil one."

Week 4.6—Friday

Title:	"Christians Pray"
First Reading:	John 17:1–26
Poetry and Wisdom:	Eccl. 5:1–6
Second Reading:	Matt. 7:7–11
Text:	Matt. 6:13—"For yours is the kingdom, and the power, and the glory forever and ever" [eighth-century insertion].

Section 5—The Creeds of the Christian Faith

Week 4.7—Saturday

Title:	"Our Confession of Faith"
First Reading:	Deut. 6:4–9; 11:1, 18–21
Poetry and Wisdom:	Ps. 119:57–72
Second Reading:	1 Cor: 15:1–11
Text:	1 Cor. 15:3–5—"For I handed on to you as of first importance what I in turn had received: that Christ died for our sins in accordance with the scriptures, and that he was buried, and that he was raised on the third day in accordance with the scriptures, and that he appeared to Cephas, then to the twelve."

Week 5.1—Sunday

Title:	"We Believe in One God"
First Reading:	Josh. 24:14–18
Poetry and Wisdom:	Ps. 14:1–6
Second Reading:	Acts 17:22–31
Text:	1 Cor. 8:6—*"For us there is one God*, the Father, from whom are all things and for whom we exist, and one Lord, Jesus Christ, through whom are all things and through whom we exist."

A. WE BELIEVE IN GOD THE FATHER

Week 5.2—Monday

Title:	"God, the Father"
First Reading:	Gen. 1:1–5; Exod. 3:13–15
Poetry and Wisdom:	Ps. 68:1–6
Second Reading:	Matt. 5:43–48; 7:21–23
Text:	1 John 3:1—"See what love the Father has given us, that we should be called children of God; and that is what we are."

Week 5.3—Tuesday

Title:	"God, the Almighty"
First Reading:	Gen. 17:1–8
Poetry and Wisdom:	Ps. 91:1–16
Second Reading:	Rev. 19:1–16
Text:	Rev. 1:8—"I am the Alpha and the Omega,' says the Lord God, who is and who was and who is to come, the Almighty."

Week 5.4—Wednesday

Title:	"God, the Maker of Heaven and Earth"
First Reading:	Gen. 1:1–31
Poetry and Wisdom:	Ps. 95:1–7
Second Reading:	Rom. 1:16–25
Text:	Gen. 1:1—"In the beginning when God created the heavens and the earth …"

Week 5.5—Thursday

Title:	"One Lord, Jesus Christ"
First Reading:	Acts 4:1–12
Poetry and Wisdom:	Ps. 118:19–29
Second Reading:	Mark 8:22–33
Text:	1 Cor. 8:6—"For us there is ... one Lord, Jesus Christ."

Week 5.6—Friday

Title:	"Jesus Christ, the Son of God"
First Reading:	Col. 1:15–20
Poetry and Wisdom:	Ps. 46:1–11
Second Reading:	John 1:1–18
Text:	John 1:18—"No one has ever seen God. It is God the only Son, who is close to the Father's heart, who has made him known."

Week 5.7—Saturday

Title:	"Jesus Christ, Our Savior"
First Reading:	Phil. 2:1–11
Poetry and Wisdom:	Ps. 49:1–9
Second Reading:	John 6:25–51
Text:	John 6:51—"I am the living bread that came down from heaven. Whoever eats of this bread will live forever; and the bread that I will give for the life of the world is my flesh."

Week 6.1—Passion Sunday

Title:	"Jesus Christ, the Son of Man"
First Reading:	Isa. 7:14; 9:2–7; 11:1–3
Poetry and Wisdom:	Job 9:1–3, 14–15, 19–20, 32–33
Second Reading:	Luke 1:26–38; 11:27–28
Text:	Luke 1:35—"The angel said to [Mary], 'The Holy Spirit will come upon you, and the power of the Most High will overshadow you; therefore the child to be born will be holy; he will be called Son of God.'"

Week 6.2—Monday

Title:	"The Passion of Christ"
First Reading:	Rom. 5:6–11
Poetry and Wisdom:	Ps. 85:1–9
Second Reading:	John 18:28–32; 19:1–42
Text:	Rom. 5:8—"God proves his love for us in that while we still were sinners Christ died for us."

Week 6.3—Tuesday

Title:	"The Resurrection of Christ"
First Reading:	1 Cor. 15:1–11
Poetry and Wisdom:	Ps. 42:1–11
Second Reading:	John 20:1–22
Text:	1 Cor. 15:3–6—"Christ died for our sins in accordance with the scriptures, and that he was buried, and that he was raised on the third day in accordance with the scriptures, and that he appeared to Cephas, then to the twelve. Then he appeared to more than five hundred brothers and sisters at one time."

Week 6.4—Wednesday

Title:	"The Ascension of Christ"
First Reading:	John 17:1–5; Matt. 28:16–20
Poetry and Wisdom:	Ps. 110:1
Second Reading:	Luke 24:44–53; Acts 1:1–11
Text:	Ps. 110:1—"The Lord says to my lord, 'Sit at my right hand until I make your enemies your footstool.'"

Week 6.5—Thursday

Title:	"The Second Coming"
First Reading:	Rev. 1:1–8
Poetry and Wisdom:	Ps. 53:1–6
Second Reading:	Matt. 24:1–31, 36
Text:	Matt. 24:30—"Then the sign of the Son of Man will appear in heaven, and then all the tribes of the earth will mourn, and they will see 'the Son of Man coming on the clouds of heaven' with power and great glory."

Week 6.6—Friday

Title: "The Judgment"

First Reading: Rom. 2:1–16

Poetry and Wisdom: Ps. 96:1–13

Second Reading: Matt. 25:1–46

Text: Matt. 16:27—"For the Son of Man is to come with his angels in the glory of his Father, and then he will repay everyone for what has been done."

Week 6.7—Saturday

Title: "The Kingdom of God"

First Reading: 2 Pet. 1:1–11

Poetry and Wisdom: Ps. 145:1–13

Second Reading: John 18:33–37

Text: Mark 1:14–15—"Jesus came to Galilee, proclaiming the good news of God, and saying, 'The time is fulfilled, and the kingdom of God has come near; repent, and believe in the good news.'"

C. WE BELIEVE IN GOD, THE HOLY SPIRIT

Week 7.1—Passion Week / Palm Sunday

Title: "The Holy Spirit"

First Reading: John 14:15–27; 16:7–15

Poetry and Wisdom: Ps. 48:1–14

Second Reading: Acts 2:1–21

Text: John 20:21–22—"Jesus said to them again, 'Peace be with you. As the Father has sent me, so I send you.' When he had said this, he breathed on them and said to them, 'Receive the Holy Spirit.'"

Week 7.2—Passion Week / Holy Monday

Title: "The Spirit Gives Life"

First Reading: Joel 2:28–32

Poetry and Wisdom: Ps. 51:1–10, 17

Second Reading: Acts 2:22–42

Text: Acts 2:38—"Peter said to them, 'Repent, and be baptized every one of you in the name of Jesus Christ so that your sins may be forgiven; and you will receive the gift of the Holy Spirit.'"

Week 7.3—*Passion Week / Holy Tuesday*

Title:	"The Holy Trinity"
First Reading:	Acts 10:1–48
Poetry and Wisdom:	Ps. 100:1–5
Second Reading:	Matt. 28:16–20
Text:	Matt. 28:19–20—"Go therefore and make disciples of all nations, baptizing them in the name of the Father and of the Son and of the Holy Spirit, and teaching them to obey everything that I have commanded you. And remember, I am with you always, to the end of the age.'"

Week 7.4—*Passion Week / Holy Wednesday*

Title:	"The Spirit and the Prophets"
First Reading:	Acts 3:17–26
Poetry and Wisdom:	Prov. 29:18
Second Reading:	Eph. 4:1–16
Text:	Heb. 1:1—"Long ago God spoke to our ancestors in many and various ways by the prophets, but in these last days he has spoken to us by a Son."

D. WE BELIEVE IN THE CATHOLIC AND APOSTOLIC CHURCH

Week 7.5—*Passion Week / Maundy Thursday*

Title:	"The Church of God"
First Reading:	John 17:13–24
Poetry and Wisdom:	Ps. 133:1–3
Second Reading:	Matt. 16:13–20
Text:	Matt. 16:18 – "You are Peter, and on this rock I will build my church, and the gates of Hades will not prevail against it."

Week 7.6—*Passion Week / Good Friday*

Title:	"Baptism and the Forgiveness of Sins"
First Reading:	Rom. 6:1–11
Poetry and Wisdom:	Ps. 130:1–6
Second Reading:	John 1:19–34
Text:	Luke 24:46–47—"Thus it is written, that the Messiah is to suffer and to rise from the dead on the third day, and that repentance and forgiveness of sins is to be proclaimed in his name to all nations, beginning from Jerusalem."

Title:	"Resurrection and Eternal Life"
First Reading:	1 Cor. 15:12–23
Poetry and Wisdom:	Job 19:13–27
Second Reading:	John 5:24–29
Text:	John 3:16—"For God so loved the world that he gave his only Son, so that everyone who believes in him may not perish but may have eternal life."

Section 6—Christ Is Risen! Hallelujah!

Week 8.1—Easter / Resurrection Sunday

Title:	"Christ Is Risen! Hallelujah!"
First Reading:	Gen. 2:4–9, 15–17
Poetry and Wisdom:	Ps. 111:1–10
Second Reading:	Mark 16:1–8; 1:1–15
Text:	Mark 1:1—"The beginning of the good news of Jesus Christ, the Son of God."